Enabling Joy

YOUR CALLING AS A LEADER

(even when you're not the boss!)

Paul F. Armstrong

First Edition

Edited by: Innovative Editing, LLC Lancaster, PA
Book Layout ©2017 BookDesignTemplates.com

Paul Armstrong / CreateSpace
1740 Wilderness Road
Lancaster, PA 17603
www.enthusaprove.com

Library of Congress Control Number: 2017917133
CreateSpace Independent Publishing Platform, North Charleston, SC

Enabling Joy/ Paul F. Armstrong. —First edition
ISBN-13: 978-1976582349
ISBN-10: 1976582342

Contents

Many people, from business associates, to authors to fellow coaches and members of clergy contributed to my understanding of enabling joy. The process of writing this book came with ups and downs and difficult choices. I was blessed to be able to rely on a large handful of wonderfully generous people who read some very rough first drafts and helped transform rambling ideas into a better story. The concept of "Faith, Humble Service and Joy" was unpacked for me in a homily by the Most Reverend Daniel Thomas, Bishop of Toledo, wherein he gave credit to a homily given by Pope John Paul II. Special warm thanks go to: Roger North, who welcomed a stranger into his office, listened, shared some honest thoughts and then gave me the courage stick with my heart; Dr. Tini, my goddaughter, whose own situation prompted me to see these ideas in a clearer light; my business partner Amanda who puts the ideas of this book into action; my diligent daughter-in-law who improved several drafts. My sincere appreciation to my bride, Diana, for her patience while I disappeared to write in quiet. I want to especially thank a beloved Visitation sister, who was instrumental in helping craft this fable and to portray these ideas with the respect due their origins. Most importantly, I thank the Holy Spirit. I pray that I've been true to His gentle and persistent guidance.

Dedicated to
James P. O'Kane (Uncle Jimmie)
He showed me the joy of a good story.

Joy is Strength.

Mother Theresa

PROLOGUE

We remember stories. That's why this guide is told as a fable. It's meant to help you see a truth you knew all along: a truth about what you're really called to do when you lead. While the story is fiction, it's not fictitious. The fable parallels a journey of discovery, a journey I took with many teams, over more than twenty years, in roles ranging from new player to facilitator to leader.

But since I understand some folks won't want to sit through a story – for reasons I can't fathom – there's also...

The QuickGuide in the back.

I get it. You're busy. And you need to figure out what to do on Monday morning. If you're in a hurry and I can't talk you into a fun fable, then go ahead and jump to the back of this book. It includes lots of references that reveal how the fable has a lot of truth baked in... so maybe you'll want to try the fable after all.

For years, I had several mandates about joy from W. Edwards Deming rattling around in my thoughts. The way I summarized his sayings in my head:

Enable joy in work.

Slowly but surely, I was able to see the amazing wisdom in his statements – but only after quiet consideration of the Creation account in Genesis. Both respected experts and my own experiments in leading teams reinforced what I learned from the Word of God.

So this book is about how to lead. It's not about leadership traits, nor is it about management. Both of those factors are critical, yes, but they're not the point of the story. With that said, I will say this on the subject.

I do believe that anytime someone is responsible for getting a group to accomplish anything, it requires both leading and managing. While these two duties are highly interconnected, they can be made distinct simply enough with the following thought:

Manage the work; lead the people.

The following parable is about several leaders, all of who are responsible for running projects. Yet they're really not the bosses of anyone assigned to their project teams. These are complicated situations, to say the least.

Yet one way or the other, they're able to discover that their job as leaders is to enable joy in work – and what that actually means on a day-to-day, project-to-project, and personality-to-personality basis.

You'll meet lots of folks in this parable. With one exception, they're good people with desirable leadership traits. But those statements or recognitions don't answer the question of what a real leader does. And my real desire is to give you some ideas on exactly that: what to DO as a leader.

Enabling joy in work resonates with a trove of evidence that's surfacing in the fields of management, leadership, biology, and neuroscience. That's nice. Yet the real power is where it's first based – in the most powerful love story of all time: the fundamental love story that frames the beliefs of billions. Yes, we're talking about the Creation story.

This is the *heart* of this fable. You'll see how as you read on. So let's jump right in!

> *"The joy of the gospel fills the hearts and lives of all who encounter Jesus. Those who accept His offer of salvation are set free from sin, sorrow, inner emptiness and loneliness. With Christ, joy is constantly born anew... I wish to encourage the Christian faithful to embark upon a new chapter of evangelization marked by this joy..." "Evangelii gaudium" by Pope Francis I, November 24, 2013*

CHAPTER 1

Trouble at Heart

Joanna drove right past her favorite coffee stand. She did it deliberately even though she was really craving her morning fix of special Ethiopian blend. After hours of pondering, she'd decided last night that maybe, just maybe, it was her caffeinated energy that was alienating her team. Her traditional cup of Joe just wasn't worth it.

After the third person on her project team quit in just the last two months, Joanna was officially desperate to figure out what was happening.

She knew the statistics. Eighty percent of people who leave their job do so not because they actually want to leave. They're simply trying to escape their boss. And as the project manager, Joanna could be considered their boss.

When the first person left the company, she ascribed the cause to all sorts of reasons other than her. The second departure took her by surprise and that's when the headaches began.

Now, it was three. Her love of finding the underlying math in any situation left her recognizing a common denominator, a factor she'd previously been able to ignore. It hurt a lot to contemplate that these folks were leaving because of her – because she wasn't leading well. As an overly driven pleaser, the guilt driven migraines were becoming a daily torture.

It all started four months ago when her company, Coeurs, decided to launch several major changes at one time.

Joanna became the team leader for setting up the new processes, including the one for the most profitable product for their most demanding customer.

She worked at a site with just over three hundred people, the largest of Coeurs' seven locations. Coeurs was a mid-sized specialty manufacturing company that had started in the medical-device arena but now supplied robotics companies, the food industry, and even some specialty items for the growing network of organic farmers.

The business made precision moving components from completely non-toxic, oil-free materials. Its facetious unofficial slogan was that it made "parts so safe, you could eat them."

By necessity, it had a longstanding deep trust with its customers.

To maintain those trust levels, sustain its strong growth, and still be able to branch into an ever-expanding spectrum of different components, the Coeurs board of directors had issued a strong challenge to CEO Tom Waldmor. They wanted him to put in place a strong, process-oriented, performance-improvement strategy for managing the company's short-term product lines – all within a year.

It was a challenge Tom had accepted with sincerity. He was an advocate of maintaining a balance between innovation in products and continual improvement in production.

That same challenge, in the mind of Joanna, was both a noble challenge and yet also was an indictment that maybe she had not been the manager she needed to be. She sensed displeasure from the board, and for the pleaser that Joanna was, this was yet another possible reason for her recent wave of migraines.

Joanna was what most companies would call a program manager. Directly responsible for leading some projects, her major role involved taking charge of aligning, prioritizing and integrating the entire portfolio's resources for her site, which had been long-since nicknamed Buggy Works. The other project leaders didn't report to her directly,

Project Management:
Defined broadly as the set of tools, techniques and skills to interdependently manage a project's costs, schedule, quality, scope, human resources, procurement, risk, communications, integration, and stakeholders. The first four of these are fairly straightforward and supported with IT tools. The others, however, involve a balance of art and science.

but they had come to consider her their leader when working together across projects.

Her role as a program manager emphasized maintaining the predictability and repeatability of performance. The mandate from the board as she understood it was a complicated mix of making processes better and yet making projects more predictable. She thought she'd enjoy the complex challenge of integrating these diverse elements, but she had been blind to the reality that it could drive her people to leave Coeurs. For the first time in years, she was experiencing migraine headaches. When they first came back, she thought it may be due to her coffee intake, but deep in her gut, she knew what really was causing them.

Performance Improvement Strategy:
Performance improvement is typically pursued using a defined set of tactics, or strategy. Common strategies focus on process improvement, variation reduction, the removal of non-value steps, standardizing, knowledge sharing, and a focus on innovation, to name a few.

How in the world had she managed to fail to please her people?

CHAPTER 2

A Perfect Problem

Joanna's site was located in the rolling hills of central Pennsylvania. It was its proximity to Amish country that had earned it the "Buggy Works" nom de plume.

Buggy Works had been a specialty machine shop that Coeurs essentially bought at a fire-sale price. As the company's newest facility, it had been equipped with 3D printers right alongside traditional shaping and forming tools. The resulting niche Coeurs had created was that it made its components with the type of techniques reminiscent of precision machining, even though it didn't work with metals.

Since the initial buyout, Buggy Works had become the go-to site for whenever new components or new processes were developed and prototyped. Therefore, the work was rarely a production run. It was much more similar to a beta version batch run. That meant the work done there could be easily translated into a project management context, while the production process was a perfect incubator for process improvements such as

Lean and Six Sigma. Tom considered Buggy Works to be the best choice to plan and test how to put the Board's challenges into practice.

Being the go-to site, Tom was especially attentive to the organizational health at Buggy Works. The latest departure from Joanna's team, a respected designer-craftsman, had not escaped Tom's attention. It made him worry that not only would he disappoint the board

Lean – *a performance improvement strategy based on eliminating waste to make your processes "lean".*

Six Sigma - *a performance improvement strategy based on eliminating variation, thereby making processes more predictable and consistent.*

and Coeurs would lose some precious talent, but that he'd burn out one of his best process improvement leaders along the way.

Tom had handpicked Joanna to fill her current role. While Coeurs wasn't big on titles, "team leader" was one that meant something: a reminder that Tom was looking for something much more than just a manager to change some processes. He needed a groundbreaker who would help change people's beliefs. He wanted people who others would follow: team leaders who knew how to tap into others' creativity while still providing worthwhile direction.

He'd hired Joanna several years ago for just that reason. And she'd consistently proved to be a competent and serving leader. At least until recently.

The way he saw it, Joanna had all the traits one would want in a leader. She was people-smart and tech-savvy. Humble without being weak. Considerate yet fair, and genuinely interested in what was best for her people. If, as the Maxwell bestseller stated, there were twenty-one irrefutable laws of leadership, Joanna demonstrated at least eighteen of them.

So why she was suddenly losing team members was a mystery he had to solve.

As quickly as possible.

CHAPTER 3

Heart of the Culture

C oeurs had been born in the late nineties when total
quality management and re-engineering had been the
popular corporate fashions.

The company's founders, a pair of artisan machinists, had
wanted to have a business that integrated W. Edwards Deming's
philosophy into every possible process, practice, procedure and
policy: "Enable joy in work." And, sure enough, since it made
consistently amazing and valuable products that medical device
manufacturers gobbled up, Coeurs was able to provide steady
and satisfying employment.

Admittedly, keeping the team engaged and contented had
been more of a natural happenstance than a reasoned strategy.
The original owners, who no longer worked at the company,
had simply set a standard of putting people in charge who could
manage the business while ensuring that Coeurs always put
people first.

Who is Deming?

W. Edwards Deming, 1900-1993, is considered by many to be the father of modern industrial quality.

A key player in the effort to increase production and quality to support WWII, Deming went to post-war Japan, where his approach was widely adopted. By the 1980s, the Japanese credited this American as the reason behind their transformation from a starving country to a world industrial power. Their top national quality award is even named in his honor.

Deming stressed improvement of the process, quoting the statistic that over 90% of the results are due to the process and the rest due to special causes, some of which are people. His "14 Points" encapsulate his advice to leaders.

He claimed that while "management is prediction," a manager's real job is to enable people to have joy in work.

Coeurs' central tenets had been built on the management mandates from Deming. The mandates were that management is a prediction and that a manager's job is to enable people to have joy in work. This latter one was a loosely understood concept.

When Coeurs was small, the leadership realized that trust thrived better when everyone knew each other's name. Taking a lesson from companies like Gore, Coeurs decided that the maximum number at a site would be three hundred. Whenever it needed to grow, it simply opened a new site and created a new community. While this seemed to go against economies of size, management liked how it kept each location feeling like a family: a tight-knit community.

While that seemed to enable joy in work, interestingly enough, it wasn't the real reason for employees' sense of accomplishment and purpose.

Buggy Works was the newest site, and because of its new equipment, it was actually populated to three hundred nearly from the get go. On the hallway walls were professionally framed posters of the Deming mandates. This was an ironic twist since Deming railed against meaningless slogans on the wall. Having become just a familiar piece of the interior décor, their words had lost their soul-searching impact.

Still there, they were just waiting to be acknowledged again.

CHAPTER 4

Truth Facts

J oanna was coming back from her morning meeting with the project leaders. Since she conducted her meetings on the move, it was more like a tour group. The huddle would move around the facility, sharing project and product updates while simultaneously taking in the actual advancements their teams were making. Oftentimes, they would just listen to the artisans' and designers' descriptions of how the processes were coming along.

Everyone knew Joanna would steer the tour to cover certain parts of facility, and that the tour would take exactly thirty minutes. Keeping the time limit was her promise to her team to always show respect for their own busy schedules, yet another way she tried to be a pleaser. Updates were just that: updates. So their daily tour was not about fact-finding, causal analysis or decision-making. If those were needed, another conversation would be planned.

As Joanna moved down the hallway, still craving her warm mug of Ethiopian brew, she happened to glance at a Deming placard. The recent staff departures were weighing down on her thoughts, but something in those familiar words no longer sounded so tired this time.

Today, the placard spoke directly to her in a clear and personal way.

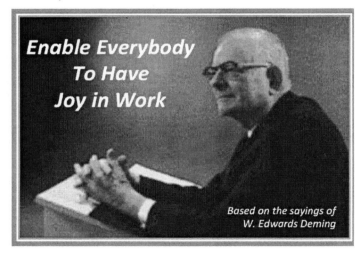

Enable Everybody To Have Joy in Work

Based on the sayings of W. Edwards Deming

It made her heart tighten as she realized she wasn't just failing to please everyone, she was failing to do this, to enable joy in work. The migraine started to make her feel nauseous.

And then it hit her. She didn't even truly understand what the mandate meant.

Joy in work. For years, Joanna had assumed that she had that term figured out. After all, she was a shining example of a servant leader. She was compassionate and caring, a people pleaser. She knew about her team's families.

Yet she now supposed that, in this time of sweeping changes at Buggy Works, her recipe for engaged, passionate, and committed employees had become insufficient. Somehow, as she led her people into the realms of project management and process improvement, she hadn't been enabling all of them to have joy in their work.

Staring at the placard, she wished someone had told her as much before this point. She wished that, somehow, someway, they had made it blatantly clear.

Though, when she went to mull it over again inside her uncaffeinated head, she supposed they had. The message had been loud and clear, no matter if they never came right out and said it. It's just that they were using a different form of communication to voice their dissatisfaction.

They were telling her with their feet.

CHAPTER 5

First Steps

With her feet out of the car, Joanna tightened the shoelaces on her boots. Reaching back, she grabbed the bag of goodies that would be her lunch and dinner for this one-day escape to her favorite hiking area in the Pocono Mountains.

A consummate journal writer, Joanna found it to be a cathartic process that helped keep her life in balance. She used it as a way to plan, examine and study her actions and decisions. Now in her early thirties, Joanna wasn't married. And getting married wasn't something she was working hard to do just then. She was a loving daughter who helped at her parents' small hobby farm, and spent lots of time with her nieces and nephews. Moreover, she was deeply faith-filled and a dynamic presence in her church, helping with mission functions and teaching in the religious education program.

In Myers-Briggs language, she clearly preferred intuitive data gathering and making relational decisions with introverted energy.

That's why, before Friday afternoon could even come to a close, she had decided to rearrange her upcoming weekend, which was a long one thanks to Labor Day. She would have normally spent it helping her parents, but she decided to take the time to herself in the woods instead.

An environmental scientist by education, Joanna loved the outdoors. Her appreciation for natural systems underscored her knack for solving complex issues in the workplace. For this day hike, she had also pulled a couple of books from the recesses of her office bookshelf and stashed them in her backpack.

Joanna was officially on a mission, with a burning question to be answered:

What in the world was joy in work?

As she locked the car in the early morning light, she paused and silently said a little prayer. She double-checked the recently repaired zipper on her vibrant, red backpack, made a visual check of her journal, and noted the charge indicator on her cell phone before slipping it into the mesh pouch on the strap.

Joanna hiked about a mile until she found a log that had been in the morning sun. Since the dew was still heavy on the fallen leaves, a dry spot was a rare find that shouldn't be taken lightly.

It seemed like a perfect moment to journal, but when she pulled out her notebook and pen, she couldn't seem to find any thoughts to capture.

So, sitting with her back to the east, she instead pulled out and opened up the yellowed pages of Deming's' *The New Economics*, a book entrusted to her by her first mentor at Coeurs. Joanna flipped through the chapters one by one, triggering memories of what she had learned several years ago.

"Enable joy in work"… What was that all about?

She refreshed her thinking on Profound Knowledge with its four elements: knowledge of variation, theory of knowledge, appreciation for a system, and psychology. Somehow, she thought to herself, that combination spelled out "joy."

In the silence of the morning, she started speaking her thoughts out loud.

"Variation: That's what we're getting better at with our Lean and Six Sigma efforts. That's what the artisans seem to really appreciate for the insights they offer. So that shouldn't be robbing their joy."

Joanna flipped the pages of the paperback rapidly, creating a sort of flipbook of Deming ideas.

"Appreciation for a System: That's always been my strong suit. Did I somehow lose sight of something about it though?"

She looked around as if the early morning forest could yield an answer. But there were only trees, trees and more trees beginning their transition for a wintery sleep.

More on Deming

*Deming proposed a model he referred to as **Profound Knowledge**. He was not at all implying that he was profound (though many think he was), but instructing us to have knowledge that makes a profound difference.*

His model has four interdependent elements:

Psychology *– We need to understand people and the interactions between people. Each of us is unique, but we're also each born with a common need for relationships, and a desire to learn and have a purpose.*

In order to encourage the positive, innate attributes of people, we must understand psychology. Deming said the purpose of his famous 14 Points was to "restore the joy in work."

Appreciation for a System *– As Deming himself put it, "A system is a network of interdependent components that work together to try to accomplish the aim of the system." For example, the players in an excellent orchestra are not there to play solos; they need not be the best players in the country. Each simply has an obligation to the system.*

He also said that "a system must have an aim . . . . . . Without an aim, there is no system." And management of a system requires knowledge of the interrelationships within it.

Knowledge About Variation *– As already mentioned, Deming said that management is prediction. We make decisions based on our interpretation of the variations we see around us.*

Variation is a given. As managers, we need to have some understanding of it to come to logical, actionable conclusions. Recognizing that, Deming classified variations as either common or special cause.

"Okay." She took the hint. "I'll leave this one open."

Then there was more flipping until she hit the theory of knowledge section at which she unconsciously wrinkled her nose.

She murmured her thoughts aloud. "Hmm, this project management effort is kind of making us be more open about what we think we know. And that risk stuff is trying to help us think of the stuff we're not sure about. Maybe that could be considered part of this theory of knowledge."

Joanna pictured all the changes she and her fellow team leaders were making to revamp almost every meeting. The goal was for everyone, not just the meeting organizer, to distinguish dialogue-learning deliberations from decision discussions.

She shook her head. "I really hope that's not the source of frustration." It seemed silly if it was. She just couldn't believe folks would quit because their meetings were clunky.

More flipping then. Joanna did stop at a few pages, though only long enough to read a paragraph or two before she closed the book and shoved it into her backpack.

"Psychology, knowledge of psychology," she pondered. "That's got to be the part about joy. Right?"

But it only took her a second before she was questioning that conclusion. Maybe it was really about all four of the elements. Then again, joy in work definitely sounded like its roots would be in psychology.

As she thought the words through, Joanna found herself scraping her boots along the leaf-littered forest floor. In the loamy, mulchy dirt below her, she could see the hair-like strands of surface roots.

As the roots go, so goes the tree.

A branch cracked near her, disrupting the random, seemingly inconsequential thought. Jerking her head to the side, she relaxed after spotting the source of the sound: a slow-moving beaver about twenty yards away. He appeared to be trying to move a branch from one place to another.

Joanna watched for a moment. A beaver at work.

Does he have joy in work?

Her years of studying nature would tell her yes. The world, at its core, was a system in balance. And that natural system had an inner contentment on par with joy. At least she thought the two should be synonymous. Maybe?

It struck her that perhaps she didn't even know what the actual definition of joy really was.

With a small shrug at both the beaver's daunting job and the magnitude of her own self-appointed task, Joanna packed her notebook away. She glanced up and noted the blaze on the tree, took mental note of her north south orientation and slid off the log.

As her boots collected the moist seeds from the low-lying grasses, her mind kept tossing around ideas about joy in work, coming back to the same question over and over again.

What is joy?

She found herself hearing the words of *Joy to the World*.

That seemed a bit crazy, it being only September and all. The first couple stanzas kept looping in her mind. As other images of the Christmas season brushed by her mind's eye, she began to hear the words in a slightly new way.

The realization of the season then reminded her that the first day of Sunday school would be next week. She knew she'd be starting with the Creation story, which at least some of the students would doubtlessly challenge, asking questions about evolution and the like. Joanna preferred to help them see this well-known Genesis account as the beginning of a love story between God and man.

Its intention was to speak to the truth, which wasn't the same as a history text full of facts. The Genesis story unveiled a mystery – a concept more expansive and awesome than could typically fit into the human mind.

It took a moment for that set of musings to collide with her previous reflections. But when it did, it brought her to a figurative and literal standstill.

In the lush green of the late summer forest, with the morning sun peering through the trees, Joanna could feel a connectedness to the world described in the Creation account and its awe-inspiring implications.

That story explained a deeper mystery.

Rather like joy.

Halfway up the mountain now, Joanna challenged herself to find a more powerful metaphor. But no matter how many word associations she played, she kept discarding them. It didn't seem like a concept she could fully grasp with regular language, and so she decided to try drawing it instead.

Up ahead, there was a switchback in the trail that featured a large rock that would make a great spot to perch on. So, scrambling up the hillside, she clambered up onto the sandstone spot, which was already a little warm to the touch in the strengthening sunlight. Sliding off her backpack, Joanna quickly unzipped the pouch and she pulled out her notebook and pen.

"Okay. No words, just a picture," she instructed herself. She took a deep breath and did her best to concentrate.

But the melody of "Joy to the World" was still quietly running through her mind, complete with little nativity scenes of stables and mangers, and the baby Jesus.

As her free hand tucked some stray hairs behind her ear, she challenged herself to focus a second time. Then she drew the first picture that came to mind to define joy.

Which was a woman changing a baby's diaper.

Apparently, her brain had circled right back to that Christmas carol after all, even though she'd tried so hard to redirect her attention.

Joanna stared at the picture in puzzlement, completely clueless about why her brain wouldn't function the way she wanted it to. Thinking that she'd simply turn the page and start again, her fingers were already bending back the sheet when she had to stop and reconsider.

She had learned through her meditative practices to show respect to ideas that seemingly had no place. It was a concept that already made sense considering something her father had told her years ago. He had likened random, seemingly inconsequential ideas to yeast. Picturing him with flour on his hands and shirt, she considered how just as a teaspoon of yeast transforms a pound of flour into fluffy bread, our tiny ideas can transform dry thoughts into delicious possibilities.

Joanna smiled as she pictured one of his homemade loaves. "Okay, Dad. If you're right, then I'm going to let this picture be my yeast."

It was a nice notion, right before she remembered all the other ingredients involved. She might have the yeast, but she still needed flour, water, salt and sugar. "Good grief!"

She stared at the picture. Joy in work. Joy to the world. A mother changing a baby's diaper.

"What does it all mean?"

She contemplated changing her nieces' and nephews' diapers, hardly a chore that anyone eagerly looked forward to. Their parents were always more than happy when Joanna volunteered, and for good reason. It wasn't just the potential smell;

it was the fact that it was one more responsibility on an already loaded list. Quite frankly, if a baby could be perfectly healthy with one movement a day, that'd be fine.

Even so, there was something to it. Some emotion associated with the act. A sense of comfort. A sense of – could she call it joy?

Joy in work?
Joy in changing a diaper?

The more she thought about it, the more she realized that, yes, there was joy involved. Not happiness necessarily, but joy. She might be holding her nose the whole time, gingerly careful about exactly how she pulled open that full diaper. Yet, all the while, there was an inner joy. Moreover, she realized, for the baby on the receiving end of the action, there would be the kind of contentment that came with a warm, dry diaper and human companionship.

The realization – the recognition – was fascinating. But it still left a very large question.

What exactly caused that joy?

CHAPTER 6

Diaper Revelation

S taring at her sketch, Joanna was tempted to draw another but decided to trust her instincts instead. Somehow, someway, this one was going to answer her quest.

Closing her notebook, she pushed her pen down the spiral spine and put it all away in favor of an apple she'd brought. Then, clenching the fruit in her teeth, she used both hands to put her pack on and slip on her sunglasses before she skittered down off the rock and headed up the slope again.

The day was beginning to warm up, but a cool breeze and scattered cloud cover was keeping it from becoming uncomfortably hot. Given the beautiful weather and the holiday weekend, it seemed surprising that there were no other hikers on the trail.

The solitude was a solace to her, and Joanna found herself thinking about her upcoming hiking and retreat vacation later in the fall.

That consideration quickly made way for what appeared to be her mind's current obsession, and with a deep cleansing breath, "let earth receive her king" played again across her consciousness. Why tunes got stuck in one's head was beyond her. What was it that made brains connect the same neurons over and over again?

Before the next line could assert itself, Joanna was back to pondering joy in work though. What gave joy to her team at Coeurs? And, strangely related to that, when did changing a diaper go from being joyful to just being a job handling someone else's poo?

What was there about diaper changing that attracted her? She never minded doing it, but also never really hoped that her nieces and nephews would spend the day needing to be changed. So, as she'd determined before, it wasn't the task itself that provided the joy. It went deeper.

Joanna pictured looking into the baby's face while she performed the task. Many times, the children would be crying as she took them to be changed. They were in discomfort and wanted someone to care for them.

She supposed that she bonded to that need; she connected with their plight and did what she could to give them relief. She made it happen – getting rid of the dirty diaper and putting on a clean one so that they knew they were loved, cared for, and comforted.

Joanna mused about that for another moment, finally deciding that the sound of her own voice might help her work it out.

"Okay. That's all well and good. I mean, everyone knows we should take care of those who can't care for themselves. But that still doesn't answer my question. I'm not a diaper changer at Coeurs; I'm a team leader."

Leader.

That's what she was, and leadership was what she provided. It's what her team relied on her for, especially during times of change. Yet she was starting to worry that the specific changes this time around – the Project Management effort, the process improvements, the Lean events, and the Six Sigma projects – were creating a ruckus and that Coeurs was possibly losing sight of how it worked.

The hill started to get steeper. The clouds had cleared, and the sun was dutifully heating up the southern slope Joanna was climbing. But that temperature change bothered her a whole lot less than when a batch of stinging nettles, high from the summer's growth, brushed against her leg just above her woolen hiking socks. She winced in pain.

She refused to let it distract her for long though when she might be onto something. Already knowing full well how easily such interruptions could derail her deep thinking, Joanna forced herself to focus on the physical path and intellectual problem.

It was a good thing too, as it made her realize that her hike might be similar to what her team was experiencing. She wanted to solve the issue, and yet she also needed to focus on the trail underfoot. Perhaps that was the source of their frustration: trying to get two things done at once.

Her feet kept moving, as did her mind, evaluating each step as it came.

Diaper changing.

Joy to the World.

Times of change.

Turning a crying baby into a happy one by first being able to connect personally and with purpose.

Creating a smile and contentment for that little person.

Giving the value of that contentment away.

Joanna felt just a whisper of clarity about where these thoughts were heading.

The trail bent sharply upward, but it had already plunged back into the trees, offering cooler air under the resulting canopy. Joanna knew from past experiences that she was now near the last of the uphill portion, even if that fact was hard to see from where she was right then.

Still in pursuit of an actionable explanation, she honed in on a new product one of the teams had worked on. The designers and artisans who'd originally come up with the idea were all given the proper respect during the subsequent building phases. And every other person involved felt like they'd been a worthwhile part of the final product, a device that had delighted their customer and made Coeurs itself a lot of money.

The team had had a clear sense of purpose and a family-like tightness, two factors that had greatly aided it with this particular product. The device had come about after a customer had made a seemingly impossible request. But this group of men and women had hatched a plan, a design and a process to pull it off anyway. And then they'd followed through.

They had, in essence, changed the diaper.

CHAPTER 7

First Test

"Thank goodness!" someone shouted cheerfully, interrupting Joanna's reverie. "We found somebody!"

Clearly part of the group of young adults coming toward her, their smiles and easy airs immediately evident, the speaker was about her age. A lanky individual, he came forward, slipping off his sweaty baseball cap.

"Hey, there," he said. "Can I bother you a moment?"

Joanna smiled back. "Sure."

"I'm Dan, one of the leaders of a local –" He stopped himself with a little laugh. "Well, semi-local youth group. I guess if we were actually local, we wouldn't be lost."

Joanna found herself chuckling. It was difficult not to feed off of his friendly vibe, but she otherwise didn't interrupt.

"We spent the night at the pull-in campsite just off route 78," he explained, "and the plan was to follow the Blue Blaze

Trail around. But I have this funny feeling we're not in Kansas anymore."

"Nope," she agreed. "Not even close."

Right at that moment, they were standing on the Red Blaze Trail, which stayed mostly on the south face. The path they wanted, meanwhile, was mostly to the north. That distinction should have been simple enough, but a lot of folks liked to take longer hikes and had, over time, worn an unmarked trail that managed to connect the two routes together.

"What landmarks have you seen so far?" She asked, then proceeded to use their answers to give them directions back to the problematic little junction that must have thrown them off. And just to really make sure they didn't get themselves lost again, she added in a little nature-related instruction about recognizing shadows. Temperatures too. "A good way to keep yourselves on track is to remember that the south face will be hot and the north will be cooler."

Cheerful though they were, the group still sighed a collective relief at her parting assurance that they'd make it just fine.

Waving goodbye a moment later, Joanna remembered her own youth groups from back when she was a teen. Just like this one, she and her friends had possessed boundless energy and good intentions – but a hopeless lack of natural orienteering talent, a problem that seemed to keep getting worse with each new generation. While cell phones these days showed them beautiful satellite views of wherever they were, they were still a bit clueless on how to find blue blaze trails.

Her rescuing efforts completed, Joanna was feeling good. Even though it had stalled her own hiking progress, the experience seemed to tie in with the whole reason she'd come out here in the first place.

Is this joy in work? This feeling of satisfaction for helping people? For a job well done?

It was an interesting concept to ponder for the next mile until she came up on one of her favorite spots. Though it was nearing midday, allowing the sun to warm the small knoll, there were enough trees around to keep the area at a comfortable temperature. That was one of the reasons why she loved the place. And it certainly didn't hurt how soft moss covered a number of the rocks, making them natural resting places.

As she settled down, she disrupted a long strand of spider silk that proceeded to defy her attempts to get it off her head. Joanna actually felt a bit of guilt that she had displeased the arachnid by ruining its hard work. Her one consolation was that it would soon start making a new one anyway.

Taking out an oat with raisin bar and balancing her water bottle on the rock, she paused for a quick prayer. And, in case inspiration decided to strike again, she pulled out her notebook as well.

Genesis of Joy

J oanna took note of the subtle peacefulness in what was
really a world of species competing and cooperating in the
rhythm of nature. As evidenced by the intricate process of
the spider spinning a daily web, nature was created to be that
complex, a point she made a mental note to tell her religious
education class.

Complex. Detailed. Smooth.

She exhaled an inaudible aaah as she thought about the
beauty of the Genesis account of creation. The cadence of the
Biblical account always captivated her. She loved being able to
recite the majestic poetic character of the Creation story. She
knew from both personal and shared experience how recounting
the ancient verses in the fireside-fashion used to tell and retell it
down through the millennia could transform the familiar words,
lending a new appreciation to God's Word.

But she also remembered how its cadence took a twist.

It made her immediately reach for her phone, fumbling to get her passcode in with only one hand, and then tapping twice to open the Bible app. Choosing the New American Bible Revised Edition version, Joanna read the results slowly, half-whispering the words of Genesis 1:25 to herself:

God made every kind of wild animal, every kind of tame animal, and every kind of thing that crawls on the ground. God saw that it was good.

The words made her smile, even as she moved on to verses 26-28, eager to read and discern the part that had prompted this reading in the first place.

Then God said: Let us make human beings in our image, after our likeness. Let them have dominion over the fish of the sea, the birds of the air, the tame animals, all the wild animals, and all the creatures that crawl on the earth.

God created mankind in his image; in the image of God he created them; male and female he created them.

God blessed them and God said to them: Be fertile and multiply; fill the earth and subdue it. Have dominion over the fish of the sea, the birds of the air, and all the living things that crawl on the earth.

For comparison and clarification purposes, Joanna switched over to the New King James Version. She scrolled down to focus on verse 26 again.

> Then God said, "Let Us make man in Our image, according to Our likeness; let them have dominion over the fish of the sea, over the birds of the air, and over the cattle, over all the earth and over every creeping thing that creeps on the earth."

On the one hand, the words "over every creeping thing that creeps upon the earth" made her lips twitch in amusement. Yet "dominion" made her pause.

Since the app included a little note icon, Joanna tapped it to dig deeper.

The sidebar note highlighted how other literature at the time used these words, words like dominion, for kings rather than persons in general. But here in Genesis, dominion was being given to man. It was not just reserved for and by God. It went on to point out this as a key difference from other prevailing religions where humans were considered to be slaves of the gods, created to do menial work for the divine pantheon.

Joanna tapped off the app to think about that note. The term "slaves of the gods" had caught her attention. It got her musing how, when our focus is on money, prestige or power, it quickly becomes our god, making us slaves to it.

That would make for another good lesson for her middle school students, she realized.

While she made a mental note of that particular concept, a wisp of a new thought had her also contemplating how working for money alone was scarily similar to being a slave to the stuff.

The wisp expanded slightly from there.

Work.
Working just for money.
Slaves of a god.
Joy in work.

Like so many insects flying around a thicket of blooming flowers, the thoughts came and went, never alighting long enough to fully settle in.

Taking a deep breath, Joanna broke the messiness of her mind by first looking into the sky and then closing her eyes.

"That dominion stuff means we're not slaves," she said out loud. "Which means God wants us to enjoy our lives, or at least have joy in life. He made us in His image; gave us free will."

She switched back to what felt like such a key word: dominion. Cathedrals all over the world were inscribed with a Latin version of that same word, "dominus," which was usually translated as "lord." Interestingly, the root, "domus," actually came from the word for home. So a better translation might be "head of the household." She played with the term in her mind. "Hmm, that's like calling someone a domestic leader."

Having dominion carried the responsibility of being the head of the home. Of providing for and protecting a family.

Joanna reread the King James phrase: "Then God said, Let Us make man in Our image, after Our likeness…" It was presented differently than God's other creative acts. Most of those sounded as if God was acting alone, which made for that twist in the cadence she'd remembered before.

God is not alone. He's connected.

It affirmed the Trinity, yes, but she now saw it in a new light as well. It could apply just as easily to enabling joy in work.

She looked back at the app, scrolling up and down through the first chapter of Genesis.

Enabling joy in work. Was that what God actually did for man instead of man having to do all the work himself? As the perfect leader, God enabled everyone with free will, creative ability and companions in life to follow His example and enable joy in work.

God led first, then he created the first leader in Adam, to whom he gave dominion and responsibility to take care of the home He had created.

Logically then, the Genesis account wasn't just the start of a love story. It was the first book in a series on how to lead, a user guide on what God wanted dominion to be.

Side Note:
Even though the responsibility of dominion over the earth was given to man, because of sin, we cannot fulfill the responsibility without the saving work Jesus did for us.

Some squealing in the distance disrupted her train of thought, complete with laughter and cries of "Get that out of here!" It sounded like her lost hikers had stumbled upon some kind of creature that wasn't popular with certain members of their troop. But considering the accompanying amusement, it couldn't have been anything dangerous, so she figured there was no reason for alarm.

Deciding to get back on the trail herself, Joanna stood and stretched. There was just a little more of her uphill climb left to tackle, and then it would be downhill the rest of the way. She'd put in a few more miles and then stop for lunch.

With almost every new step she took, her reflections took her down one philosophical trail after another. Did they answer how to be a better team leader? Did they help explain what enabling joy in work was all about? Had she figured out a new way to see the Creation story? Could this help her with keeping her team engaged? To keep them from leaving Coeurs? Could this help with all those changes due to project management and process improvement? And what in the world did any of it have to do with that picture of changing a diaper?

The mountain trail finally began to level off as it reached the summit, and she began looking for a spot to kick back, not to mention record at least some of her mental pathways. She was dying to get it solidified as much and as soon as possible.

Once she found a likely resting place, Joanna balanced the notebook on her knees and just began to brainstorm, putting notes on the page in the shape of a diagram.

She thought of the interruption of her solitude by the lost youth group. How could there be joy in being disrupted? In being bothered?

But was it really a bother? Really, she'd felt connected to them, since there had been a time not so very long ago that she'd been in their shoes. Besides, there was joy in having a way to be of value: to create a solution for others. A joy in them understanding and appreciating it, and in her solution contributing to their relief.

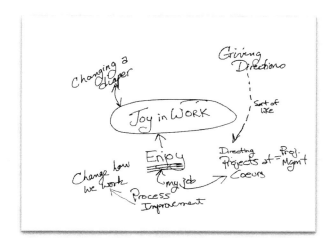

She scribbled down three more terms: Connect. Create. Contribute.

Joanna stared down at them for several seconds. She was immediately fond of the words, but she didn't know why. She'd always enjoyed poetic devices when she wrote, so she won-

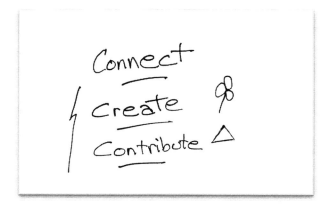

dered if she was seduced by their alliteration.

No. This is about something better than that.

In the end, she opted, as she did with many of life's puzzles, to just have faith. It might be blind or naively optimistic, but she decided to just believe the words could actually be the key she was looking for.

"After all," she blurted out loud, as if she needed to explicitly hear some reassurance, "they're inspired by the Creation account, random chance, the beauty of nature – and, in a funny way, dirty diapers."

How could she not trust that kind of inspiration?

It was an entertaining way of regarding everything, and she had already decided to go with it. But there still was the question of what to do with it all on Tuesday at Coeurs.

Joanna took out a Sharpie, ripped out a journal page and, in thick red ink, rewrote, "Connect. Create. Contribute." Then, pulling out the extra hair scrunchie she kept in her backpack, she secured the note to her water bottle.

As soon as that was accomplished, a sense of relaxation flooded her spirit – and her soul. She could feel her shoulders fall and her spine loosen, as if everything was already taken care of. In addition, she noted that she was migraine free.

The way her senses had come to rest, Joanna couldn't help but think that this particular journey could very well be downhill from there.

CHAPTER 9

Note on a Bottle

"Good morning, Joanna!"
Striding out of the parking lot on her way to the building Tuesday morning, Joanna paused to let Dayzie catch up for more than one reason.

Dayzie was her key to implementing the changes her team needed to make. The woman was pretty much everything one wouldn't associate with a young lady of that name. It was true she was a high-energy, creative engineer who loved the innovative side of Coeurs. But her real talent was helping teams be proficient in managing costs, scopes, schedules and quality levels. More importantly, Dayzie helped other leaders see the value in installing explicit plans and strategies for proper risk communication and pulling in other team players as needed.

Joanna did her best to listen as they walked briskly across the lot. But Dayzie was rapid-firing a series of anecdotal bits of information, which rather felt like coloring in a paint-by-numbers picture. Joanna wished that she had a better affinity for lists of facts and sort of envied Dayzie's ability to keep so many at the tip of her fingers.

From what she could understand, the numbers were showing that their keystone project was wallowing. It wasn't that there was a shortage of good ideas or talent. But there was a shortage of productivity and morale. Despite the fast pace of her delivery, Dayzie's voice carried a timbre of somberness like a prophet of doom as she summarized how the team was having similar issues to the ones the three people who'd left had related.

Joanna was busy processing all of that when Dayzie took a quick breath in and stared at her, her eyebrows drawn down in puzzlement.

"Where in the world is your coffee?" she asked, pointing to the water bottle Joanna was carrying instead. "And why's there a note attached? Is that a reminder to buy coffee?"

That last question was a joke, Joanna recognized. Her colleague's sense of humor came from her engineering background, so her facetiousness always had a matter-of-factness to it. Yet it was always accompanied by a ready smile and frequent laugh that made Dayzie easy to be around.

Joanna looked down at the bottle, having forgotten it was even there. "Oh yeah. That. It's just a note to myself."

At first, she thought she'd just end the answer there. But Dayzie was always up for a new idea or a clever twist on old ideas, and a sounding board didn't seem like such a bad thing right then and there. Plus, Joanna was planning on talking to her anyway. Why not start now?

First though, she wanted to address that wallowing project.

"I'll tell you about it in a bit," she amended. "What are your thoughts about our favorite project though?"

Dayzie sighed. "I think the team's still struggling with identifying and mitigating risks."

She went on to refresh Joanna's memory on the risk management templates she herself had created. They were meant to make the whole process easier and more traceable. The way Dayzie saw it; they were easy to use, complete with reminders on who to consult about what for various risk categories.

"Besides," she added, "Andrew has the team on a consistent schedule to improve the process. If you ask me, this should be the happiest, most productive team on site."

"But it's not?" The question wasn't really a question though, and with that realization, came the pounding of yet another migraine.

"It's not," Dayzie confirmed.

Joanna glanced at her water bottle, thinking out loud without even realizing that she'd vocalized her thoughts. "How do I bring joy to their world?"

"Huh?"

Dayzie's voice snapped Joanna out of her reverie, and she shook her head sheepishly. "Sorry about that. Don't mind me." She forced herself to focus on the immediate, at least for the moment. "Let's chat about this later after the morning updates. Oh, and did you know Tom's coming by later this afternoon?"

Dayzie nodded, and they parted ways inside the building to get their safety glasses from their respective rooms. It was mandatory for their morning update walk.

Even as she slid hers on, Joanna was hatching a plan.

She'd just plunge in and share her thoughts with the group this afternoon. She knew Tom was here to check on some product lines, but his schedule should allow him to have an hour or so to get together. Besides, she also knew the recent employee losses were weighing heavy on his mind, and she needed to not dodge the issue.

Dayzie and Andrew should be there too when she addressed it, and so she made sure to tap them both on the shoulders as soon as the morning update was over. After making a joke about going sans coffee for a while – and how they'd have to get used to the non-caffeinated version of her – Joanna explained how the personnel situation was weighing on her mind and how seriously she was taking it.

The two of them were a bit taken aback by the admission, but both agreed to keep their schedules flexible for whenever she could get ahold of Tom.

It wasn't until they left that Joanna looked at that note on her water bottle again, the sight suddenly making her panic.

What was she thinking? How would she share this crazy idea with her boss? She'd come up with it while humming *Joy to the World* and drawing pictures of babies getting their diapers changed, for crying out loud! She took a sip, finding the water much less satisfying that her normal coffee fix. She pictured the others whom she'd talk to about this. Telling Dayzie was easy. The others? Not so much.

After a pep talk to herself in an empty stairwell, she went down to talk with Megan, the Project Leader for their keystone project. Megan was a brilliant engineer from Purdue with a background in aerospace and a passion for math. Always looking for the underlying math in any project dynamics she got ahold of, she was uncannily realistic in her estimates for task schedules.

To Joanna, the soft-spoken but firm woman was the perfect leader for this keystone project.

As Joanna walked into the work area, Megan gave her a look that spoke volumes. It wasn't quite a look of desperation, but it did hold a definite degree of exasperation and maybe even bewilderment.

"You okay there?" Joanna asked.

Seeming like she wanted to drop her head on the desk and moan, Megan managed a smile instead. "One of my best designers is talking about leaving," she explained. "He's been offered another job with great pay and a shorter commute."

Joanna grimaced in sympathy even while she recognized the statements for the opening they were.

"This job market is just getting too competitive," Megan added.

"Is it really the job market?" Joanna gently pressed.

"What do you mean?"

"Well," she offered. "I've lost three people myself in recent months, so I don't say this lightly. But maybe we should start examining why employees are looking around in the first place."

Megan blinked.

Joanna grimaced. "Statistics say the reason why 80% of people shop around like that is because of the individuals they work with – leaders in particular – not because of the work or pay or commute."

Megan's reaction was a vivid wince. "Way to make me feel worse there."

"Sorry," Joanna offered, very much meaning it.

"But," Megan went on, "as much I don't want to accept it, my inner math geek's telling me to pay attention to a figure as high as 80%."

"I'm going to have a roundtable session with Tom, Dayzie and Andrew," Joanna offered, "and I'd really like you to be there too."

She could tell as soon as the words left her mouth that Megan wasn't exactly thrilled about it. Mondays – or, in this case, Tuesday – were usually pretty regimented for her. But a second later, maybe two, she was nodding her head to indicate that, yes, she'd be there too.

"I have a meeting with him today anyway," she relented. "Maybe we could jump into your conversation right after that?"

"That sounds great to me," Joanna told her. "And thank you. This really means a lot."

CHAPTER 10

Diaper Dialogues

Joanna could hear them before she saw them. She'd arrived at the agreed team room five minutes earlier to claim a spot and get herself organized: journal, notes, water bottle, thoughts and all. Just a second ago, she'd found herself wondering if she should write out some of those thoughts on the whiteboard to her right. But she supposed it was too late now. She would have to work with what she had.

"I can take a look into that when I get back," Tom was saying, right before he and Megan appeared in the doorway to the room that Joanna had reserved.

Dayzie was the next one in, holding a cup of coffee, which she raised in salute in good-natured ribbing. And Andrew was right behind her, his hands clearly in need of a sink and soap.

Andrew was always one to roll up his sleeves with the artisan machinists, helping them tinker with their jigs in pursuit of improving the process.

Joanna was already feeling nervous before they all sat down. The fact that they proceeded to give her their full attention, exactly as she'd intended, didn't release a single stomach butterfly, and definitely didn't ease her migraine.

"Thanks for scheduling this into your day," she began a little awkwardly. "I'm just going to jump right into some hot water here."

Nobody smiled at her, but there was a sense of open concern about them that helped her feel at least a little more at ease. "We all know we've been seeing or hearing about our best folks wanting to leave. Frankly, I'm worried that we team leaders aren't providing the right direction. Or maybe I should say sufficient direction instead."

If anything, Tom was starting to look a little relieved, she noticed. It made her wonder whether he'd been trying to think of a way to schedule a meeting with her.

"I'm saying this predominantly about myself," Joanna acknowledged. "But we've had three great people leave in just a few months, and another one is apparently on the brink." She paused just long enough to let that sink in. "I'd like to pretend it's just normal turnover or that some charming force is out there luring employees away. But everything I read makes it clear that the primary reason folks leave is because of their managers, not their jobs."

That got frowns around the table – not of disagreement but of distaste or chagrin.

"I gave this a lot of thought after I reread one of the signs on our wall that we all pass all the time. It's the one that says our job as leaders is to enable our people to have joy in work."

ENABLING JOY • 61

Joanna raised her hands in chagrin. "Embarrassingly, I realized I couldn't really give myself an explanation of what joy in work is. I knew it wasn't the same as happy. I knew it wasn't about making this some sort of funhouse."

Tom looked like he wanted to say something, but if that was the case, he kept it to himself.

"That bothered me," Joanna shared. "But I knew if I was enabling joy – whatever that means – then folks wouldn't be leaving."

"So I decided that I needed to figure out what in the world it meant."

The more she got into the presentation, the more she was feeling relaxed. This was the right thing to do, regardless of how it was taken. Plus, she could sense a growing aura of hope among her boss and colleagues; maybe they thought she was onto something too.

"I went on a hike this weekend and thought the concept over." She smiled at the memories. "Admittedly, I was distract-ed by lots of other thoughts and some spectacular scenery, but I did come up with some ideas I'd like to share." The next line warranted an added note of caution. "Not saying I have an an-swer yet. It's more like the result of some nature influenced brainstorming and reflection."

"That's a good place to start," Tom assured.

With a responding nod his way, she reached for the journal. "This is what I came up with when I challenged myself to have a pictorial definition rather than a verbal one."

And then she held it up: that image of the changing table.

Dayzie wrinkled her brow.

Megan looked pensive.

Andrew sort of shrugged.

And Tom looked thoughtful, which wasn't surprising. His biggest talent was his ability to think deeply about a lot of things, from bike riding to beer making to running Coeurs.

Joanna pressed on. "Don't worry. After my pen came off the paper, I was as puzzled as you. I thought it might be because *Joy to the World* was stuck in my head for some reason."

Her self-deprecating smirk got a chuckle or two, which she seized as a good sign.

"As I bounced this around, I thought about a lot of things: what Deming taught, what that Christmas carol could really mean, and what is it about changing messy diapers that has anything to do with joy in work."

Andrew looked up from his text that just came in and actually leaned in a little while she selected her next words.

"And then it hit me," Joanna obliged. "As human beings, we have an array of needs we have to satisfy. We've probably all learned about Maslow's hierarchy of needs. I can't recite it off the top of my head, but I do remember that there are basic physiological needs and higher-order needs."

Maslow's Hierarchy of Needs – A Quick Overview

Abraham Maslow, an American psychologist, looked at needs from a hierarchical perspective. Listed from basic to higher order, they are:
Physiological (food, sleep)
Safety (security of body, health, employment)
Belongingness (friendship, family)
Esteem (confidence achievement, respect)
Self-Actualization (morality, creativity, problem solving)
Self-Transcendence

Usually depicted with a pyramid graphic with basic needs as the foundation and self-actualization being the apex.

She placed special emphasis on her next statement. "It's the higher-order ones that I think are connected to joy in work. And I think those are the ones that really motivate us."

That got three out of four indications of agreement, which furthered her own excitement about the topic – and the breakthrough waiting to be claimed.

"Deming always talked about intrinsic motivation and how it wasn't about motivating people so much as removing the barriers to their motivation."

Megan spoke up then. "So you're thinking the reason these folks left can be explained with this Deming joy in work stuff? If not, then I'm really confused where you're going with this conversation."

Joanna wasn't offended. "Yes, that's where I'm going. It dawned on me that if I were enabling people to have joy in work, they wouldn't be leaving. So since they were leaving, I must not be enabling joy."

She knew Megan would latch onto the if-then logic. Now hopefully, she'd be able to follow her next train of thought too.

Joanna swung her note-scrunchied water bottle onto the table. "I'm not going to share how this really came to me right now, but let's just say I was also doing some church work in my mind when I was trying to think this problem through."

Dayzie twitched in curiosity. Everyone else just kept listening.

"Joy in work is when leaders help us **connect** with the purpose and people, **create** something of value for them or that purpose, and then **contribute** that value – to put it into action."

This time, Dayzie nodded in agreement. "I see that. I mean, lets' face it: One of our biggest fears is being alone or not connected. We're not sled dogs; we have an inner drive to have a purpose, or, as you put it, to create value and make a difference with that value."

Like usual, Dayzie was speaking fairly fast, but Joanna didn't mind. She was more than happy for the contribution.

Tom chimed in too. "So you're saying our people leaving is evidence that we're not living up to the philosophy we claim to live by. I get that, and I appreciate how you challenged yourself to come up with an operational definition." His expression went from intrigued to confused in the very next breath though. "But I'm not following the changing-diapers part. Could you explain that again?"

So Joanna expanded on how diaper changing could be such a stinky job; how we don't wake up hoping to change one. Yet we get a sense of accomplishment – a glimmer of joy – when we do because we connect with a purpose and a person while creating value and immediately contributing it to a recipient.

Tom and Dayzie both reacted well to that explanation.

Megan's response, however, wasn't so enthusiastic. "Okay, so what does this do for me?" she asked. "I'm leading a tough project, the world is changing all around me, and we've got project-management stuff we're learning and process improvement standing up production." Her expression was weary. "It seems like a perfect breeding ground for frustration, and it shows. There's no end to the diapers, and the baby is still crying."

"Bingo." Joanna gave her a sympathetic smile. "But that's why this is so helpful. With a crying baby, I can work through a series of questions: Is she hungry, wet, sleepy or just needs to feel my love? And now we have a similar checklist of 'connect, create, contribute', to go to when we're wondering what to do as a team leader."

Feeling her thoughts coming together so much more solidly, she spoke more resolutely to the other three participants. "I completely agree with Megan. We are in a turbulent time. It's the perfect breeding ground for frustration. But face it: It's in times of change that leadership is most critical because the direction is so cloudy."

Megan seemed relieved at the statements, as if she'd been expecting to be put down for her negativity.

"When things are so up in the air, our people are most apt to feel disconnected, to think they won't be able to create value." Joanna tucked some hair behind her ear without even realizing she did. "When we spend so much time improving or managing stuff, it blurs their view that we'll ever get stuff out the door. Or, put another way, they might start wondering if they'll never see their value get contributed to our customers."

An impish grin started to emerge on Andrew, a telltale sign that his penchant for challenging every theory was in high gear.

He stood up to speak, moving over to the whiteboard and picking up one of the markers as he did. "Okay, Joanna. I see what you're saying, and it sounds cool. So let's give it a little test."

She was all ears.

"I didn't go on a hike to think over our people-leaving problem," he continued. "But I did read a book by Lencioni – that 'five dysfunctions of a team' guy – called *The Three Signs of a Miserable Job*. It's a great book, I think he's spot on, and I'd like to see if the two of you are saying the same thing."

Joanna steepled her fingers as a chin rest, eager to see where he was going.

Apparently happy to oblige, he scribbled for their benefit as he spoke. "Lencioni claims that the indicators of a miserable job are anonymity, irrelevance and immeasurable." All three words went up on the whiteboard. "Now, anonymity makes sense. It's sort of like being unconnected. And irrelevance seems to resonate with creating value. Because if I can't create value, I feel irrelevant."

He put a big, fat question mark after the last term though. "The last one, I'll admit, has me stuck. I'm not seeing how 'immeasurable' and 'contribute' link up."

REASONS TO QUIT

Anonymity ⟶ UN-CONNECTED

Irrelevance ⟶ Can't Create Value

Immeasureable ⟶ ?

Tom shook his head. "No, it makes sense to me. When I see a satisfied customer – when I see a positive profit and loss statement – I know we've contributed value. The measure is the proof of that contribution. Plus, it gives us a way to re-connect to the purpose and create more value the next time around."

Dayzie eagerly picked up from there. "Yeah, that contribute part seems obvious to me. Heck, lots of companies call their non-supervisor people 'individual contributors.' We want them to contribute and, hopefully, so do they."

Unoffended by her delivery, Andrew tilted his head in thoughtful agreement. "Hadn't thought of that. I think I was associating the word with stuff like charity contributions." Stroking his beard, he went back to the table to sit down. "Ok. Your connect, create, and contribute are holding water for me. Not sure what I'm going to do with this whole thing, but I like it."

Joanna took over again. "I'm not sure I know what to do with it either, but this is a start. Thank you so much for being patient while I used you all as a sounding board. I couldn't get my head completely around this on my own."

She stood up. "I am thinking that there's a way we can weave this into our thinking at least: use it as a filter for how to make decisions, or, more importantly, how to evaluate how thoroughly we're doing our job of enabling people to have joy in work."

Tom stood up too, with the three others following his lead. "For the record, I appreciate that all of you are taking our personnel problem seriously. And I think we're onto something. For the time being, let's just try employing it ourselves." His lips twitched upward. "But if we see some real improvement, this could be a great way of helping all our team leaders."

Glancing down at his watch, he straightened up a little further in acceptance of the time. "I need to head off to the airport, but I'm glad we had this talk."

That effectively ended the meeting, leaving people to get back to their regular schedules. But Dayzie pointedly waited for Joanna to finish picking up her notes.

Straightening up, Joanna smiled. "What's up?"

Dayzie pointed at the water bottle still sitting on the table. "I know you said you weren't going to get into the details, but I'd really like to know how this came to you. If you don't mind, I mean."

"There's no getting anything by you, is there?" Joanna gave Dayzie a smile full of appreciation and respect. Waving dismissively with her free hand, she continued, "I was just trying to save time there, not be mysterious or anything like that. It happened when I was contemplating the Creation story."

The simple statement earned her a confused look.

"When I was reading the part about God creating man, the words really jumped out at me. All of a sudden, I had a whole new understanding of what God really provided when He gave man dominion." She reached for her water bottle. "I'd be curious to know what the passage says to you."

Dayzie nodded thoughtfully. "I'd like to do that. That might make this whole idea come to me in a more meaningful light."

"That sounds great to me," Joanna told her. "And thank you. This really means a lot."

CHAPTER 11

Risk and Joy

Wednesday morning, walking toward the office's small kitchenette, Megan couldn't help but catch the animated conversation coming out of it.

"I'm telling you," someone was saying, "if there's one more thing that gets shoved down our throats, I'm going to take my talents elsewhere. I can't stand how much other stuff we need to do just to do our work!"

She toyed with the thought to just stay clear, but decided that easing in might be better. So she made like she'd been planning to walk in there all along.

Rod, her lead designer, was the first to notice her as he replaced the coffee pot. "G'morning Megan," he said pointedly and quickly drew the mug to his mouth. It was a clear sign that he wasn't really in the mood for niceties.

"Hey there," she replied, wondering how she should proceed.

Fortunately, he made it easy for her. His ire exceeded his desire for coffee and putting his mug on the table, his hands went up into a flail of surrendering motions. "We're trying to get our heads around what exactly we need to do first. We're implementing all this project management stuff, and, quite frankly, it seems like a lot of paperwork to document what we've always done anyway."

Megan wouldn't disagree with that. He was only voicing her own thoughts.

"I mean, it feels like we're spending most of our time trying to prevent *disasters*" – he made air quotes to emphasize his contempt for the board of directors' concern – "than actually doing our job."

Now, that part, she couldn't help but take issue with.

One of Megan's strong suits was her meticulous attention to detail and cautious, well-considered approach to anything new. Risk management was the perfect tool for her to document and account for predictable project variables: how they could flop, fail, or otherwise turn around and bite you.

Of all the projects that initiated risk management, Megan's was the most thorough approach, and she was normally

Risk Management Quick Note *Risk Management (RM) is on of the bodies of Project Management and a science in its own right. RM is practiced to identify, assess, mitigate, plan and review all the ways a given project or plan can go awry. Risk is a function of both likelihood of an event and the severity of the event's consequences. Common tools include risk registers, databases, and matrices. When RM is practiced well, it provides a disciplined way to prepare well for the future; when not practiced well, conversations become 'monster in the closet' emotional events.*

proud of how intensely they had put together the register.

So hearing it trashed so succinctly left her feeling torn. She respected Rod, and he was a key player. But she'd created the very tool he was trashing to make him and the rest of her team happy.

Megan told herself to think about it before she reacted, particularly when this was the second person to express frustration. "Okay," she said, sounding rather stiff even to her own ears. "Let me process that and get back to you."

He didn't look appeased, and snatched up his mug and took a sip.

"I promise," she added. "I'm not putting you off. I just want to give you a worthwhile answer."

Walking away, she thought back to yesterday's conversation. Megan still couldn't really get her head around how to use those terms Joanna had come up with, but she was willing to try again if for no other reason than she had no idea what else to do.

She found herself an empty team room and sketched a mixture of words and curves across the board.

She stared at it for a while, then scribbled some more and paused again. Thoughts raced through her mind.

So Rod is frustrated. But if Joanna is on to something, then the reason's right here.

Maybe all that risk management stuff was keeping him from creating their product, or at least telling him subconsciously that they wouldn't get it done. Maybe it was telling him they wouldn't be able to deliver or contribute.

She could see either being true. Rod was a can-do kind of guy, and she'd been pushing him to focus on all the ways he "couldn't do." Yet addressing their risks was critical.

A head poked in around the door. "Megan, we need you to take a look at something. Do you have a minute?"

She looked at her watch, then checked the daily schedule on her tablet.

She could squeeze in a minute.

"I'll be right there," she replied. Taking a photo with her tablet, she grabbed the eraser and soon the board was empty. The image though was still vividly on her mind, waiting for the next opportunity to make more sense of all this.

CHAPTER 12

Curves of Joy

Megan, pointing to the Gantt chart on her laptop screen, was animated as she explained to Dayzie, "I'm thinking we should get that delivery in time for Mike to get those pieces made, and that should keep us on schedule."

Dayzie had stopped by her office for an update, but Megan figured she'd use this as an opportunity to talk through her thoughts. She shifted her focus from the laptop to Dayzie, sharing what Rod had told her yesterday.

Dayzie listened carefully the whole way through. "Yeah, I'm starting to hear a lot of that. I think we're finding that folks just don't want to change. I've wondered if we need to have some sort of training to show how project management is better in the long run, even if it looks like more work in the short run."

She ended her thought by wiping a tired hand across her face. "Part of me just wants to say 'deal with it.' But I don't think that's a good long-term approach."

Megan knew her eyes were showing she agreed. "Well, I decided to see if I could make sense of what Joanna was talking about on Tuesday. I have some ideas – nothing I can run with yet – but if you've got a minute, I'd like to run it by you."

At the mention of a potential light at the end of the tunnel, Dayzie's expression broke into one of optimistic anticipation.

Megan flipped the project schedule over to reveal the blank side. "Remember when Joanna was talking and then Andrew mentioned that book? Well, it made me think about Deming and how he wrote about motivating employees. I never thought he was referring to Maslow." She tapped her fingers against the desk. "Somehow, I recall this other guy, Herzberg, influencing his philosophy." Megan began sketching on the blank sheet.

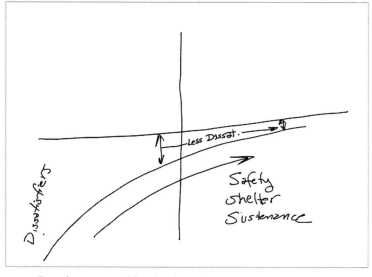

Dayzie was watching her intently.

"Herzberg wrote a famous article for *Harvard Business Review*. I think it was called something like 'How Do We Motivate Employees.' In any case, I remember it because I was able to think of it this way."

Her hand flashing across the blank schedule, she continued. "A person needs to have certain physiological needs met. They include the reason we work – to get paid so we can eat and have a house. I remember it by three S's: safety, shelter, and sustenance."

Her marker was still moving. "What I really liked about Herzberg, and why I'm showing it with this bottom curve" – she paused long enough to point out the line in question – "is that he calls these factors dissatisfiers. The more we take care of them, the less dissatisfied we are."

"Interesting," Dayzie inserted.

"Right?" Megan gestured in agreement. "That's the key point. It's not that we become motivated with more pay or benefits; we just become less dissatisfied. We get these factors to a point where they are sort of off the table."

It felt good to talk this through, she half-realized, even while she pursued it further. "I think of it as this flattening region of my curve. The critical part of his theory is what I just said: that more pay isn't motivational, it just reduces dissatisfaction. If we don't have what we think we need or if any of the S's drop, then we become more dissatisfied, not really unmotivated."

Dayzie's hand was twitching like she wished she could be taking notes.

"There's a cool YouTube video by Dan Pink. It might be on TED too. But in any case, he has some really startling statistics on the subject."

Megan couldn't let herself slow down, even though she could see that Dayzie was itching to scribble on the same sheet – not if she wanted to get it all out well. "Now, Herzberg talks about what he calls motivators, which I've designated

TED talks
TED is a media organization that posts talks online for free distribution, under the slogan "ideas worth sharing." TED was founded in 1984 as a conference and has been held annually since 1990.

with this upper curve." She pointed that one out even if Dayzie wasn't necessarily looking. "They rather build on themselves. Quite frankly, I never could grasp them very well – all of that stuff about purpose and job design. But, when I was listening to Joanna yesterday, it dawned on me that her three C's are the top curve."

Megan looked over at Dayzie, who had now taken out a tablet and was busy writing, nodding in thought. So she was still listening even while she took notes.

"Ok...three C's, three S's, that's all kind of crazy coincidence." Megan shot Dayzie a quick look indicating she was almost embarrassed by the alliterations, but then continued. "While these S's give us diminishing returns, then, if my interpretation of Herzberg is correct, using the connect, create, contribute ideas should give us increasing returns."

Dayzie's pen flourished a few more times, and then she looked up, visibly excited. "I think you've got something here!"

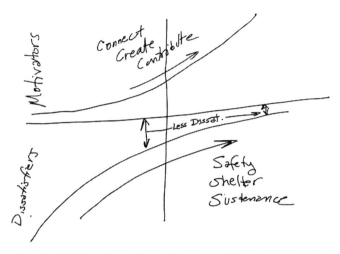

"Really?" All of a sudden, Megan felt like she needed that extra touch of confirmation that she wasn't chasing a wild goose.

"Really!" Dayzie started speaking faster. "Let's say dissatisfaction is like 'project concern,' you know, like all those issues that cause us to be worried about project success. And let's say your motivation is like 'project excitement' – no, let's try 'joy.'" She rushed on with a contagious level of enthusiasm. "Now, think about this. We're dumping lots of change onto our folks, and that probably threatens how they feel connected, how they can create, and how they contribute. We're shaking up the status quo, which makes them see an unknown monster in the closet. In other words, we're taking the top curve right off."

Megan wondered if she should be taking notes now.

"And then," Dayzie went on, "we think we're fixing that by dwelling on the bottom curve. Worse still is this risk-management stuff, which also follows the bottom curve and spends our energy on minimizing bad stuff, not maximizing good stuff. As a result, I think Rod and others are frustrated because we really took the top curve off the table."

That made Megan wince. "Are you telling me I've been doing it wrong?"

Dayzie shook her head so tightly it was almost a shudder. "It's a balance thing, not really a matter of right and

Intrinsic Motivation: How Deming Has It Right

Dan Pink, author of DRIVE: The Surprising Truth About What Motivates Us, has a fascinating whiteboard animated video that concisely explains how extrinsic rewards, like bonuses, paid vacations, etc., only result in more productivity for menial, simple tasks. Using these extrinsic motivators for tasks that require cognitive or creative skills actually backfires; productivity gets worse. This fits Alfie Kohn's research as reported in Punished by Rewards, a book often cited by Deming. Kohn's work and Pink's work help illuminate what Deming refers to when he emphasizes removing barriers to intrinsic motivation.

wrong. I think we tipped the scale too much on the lower curve, and at a time when everyone's already confused about the future."

Still feeling rather bad though, Megan sighed. "This all sounds good in theory, but I keep going back to the same problem. I just don't know where to take it."

Dayzie paused. "I'm not sure either, but between you and Joanna, you've got me seeing this situation in a whole new light." She stood up. "I gotta run, but thanks for sharing!"

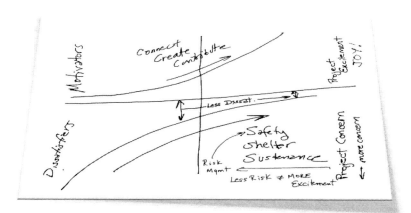

CHAPTER 13

Kitchen Counter Clarity

Reaching into the refrigerator, Dayzie gently squeezed the spongy ball with its wax paper cover. "Perfect."

She had made the focaccia dough the day before and was now ready to transform it into the main attraction for family dinner. As she rolled it out and made indents with her fingertips, she got to thinking.

Back when she first joined Coeurs, she'd had dreams of being a power woman. Full of ambition, talent and education, she had figured that she'd be in a managerial office before she turned thirty.

Yet when Tom Waldmor took over, he had set about playing down the whole hierarchy. In fact, he'd flattened the structure and was now pushing project management instead.

Dayzie loved the challenge of managing a project. But the definitions and expectations that went with this new work environment were confusing. On the one hand, she was supposed to get folks to follow her lead. Yet as a mere project manager, she lacked the proper authority to really enforce what she needed to enforce. Nobody on her team actually worked for her in a chain-of-command sense.

Tom had pretty much gotten rid of titles and classic organization charts. In her gut, Dayzie did like how he'd transformed the company; but she was still looking for a functional way to lead without a functional title to go with that task.

Joanna's slant the other day about enabling joy seemed like it might possibly answer that very question. There was just one catch: Dayzie still had to wrap her mind around what those two words together really meant.

She thought about what Joanna had interpreted from the Creation account in Genesis. A Christian as well, Dayzie respected her colleague's faith, but she also liked stepping back and taking her own look at things.

That's why she'd already gone digging for the original Hebrew or Greek words used in the passage Joanna had cited. The original Hebrew word translated as "rule," was "radah," which meant to have dominion, rule, or subjugation over something.

That had led her to wonder about the exact meaning of dominion, so she looked into radah a little further. It was

Quick Note

Dayzie's verses are based on the New King James Version of the Bible.

apparently used throughout the Bible for kings who held positional power, such as King Solomon in 1Kings 4:24. And as Daniel 2:21 and Romans 13:1-2 made clear, the positional power was given by God.

It seems the word referred to the responsibility of kings, chiefs, and officers to be representatives of the one who first gave them that authority – a concept that was further highlighted in Matthew 25:14-30. Meanwhile, James 3:1 made it clear that leaders were held to a higher standard than followers.

Ever since reading that last revelation, Dayzie had been feeling off-and-on twinges in her stomach. Because, the way she figured it, that higher standard then applied to her. It wasn't just the company that had given her responsibility over people and resources. God was also trusting that she, as the delegated person, would be a good steward – a good, serving leader.

Her mind took a relevant bunny trail as she stared at the kitchen counter, realizing that making a dinner could be considered a chore just as much as any of her tasks at work. Yet she didn't see it that way. No matter whether she was preparing an easy meal of spaghetti or spending time to make her special bacon-wrapped pork tenderloin, she always enjoyed doing it.

It was joy in what could be interpreted as work.

Why?

Joanna's words scrolled across her consciousness, bringing the answer with it. That diaper. It was like that diaper, though admittedly less smelly. She connected with her family through her meal preparations, creating value. It didn't matter if it was an easy meal of spaghetti or the tedious effort involved in a bacon-wrapped tenderloin. It was a joy to be able to provide it.

So why aren't we doing that at Coeurs?

Why was this project management effort in particular causing so much angst? She was implementing it the way any other change should be managed, spelling out the vision, starting pilots, and keeping folks from getting worried.

A haunting thought followed, growing from a nagging suspicion until it was a full-blown conscious realization that she had to get out of her head

"Oh my word!" As if she were talking to a crowd, her hands came out of the dough and made a supplicating gesture. "That's what I'm doing wrong. That's what we're all doing wrong. We forgot what our jobs are!"

Her five-year-old son careened into the kitchen while that realization was still tingling through her body.

"What are you saying, Mommy?"

"Oh, nothing dear," she assured. "Just talking to myself."

But even as the words came out of her mouth, she told herself that it was far from nothing. It was something. Something big. Something really cool.

Dayzie looked at her son again. He was standing there, his focus on her dough-laden fingers. She put in a few indents in a teasing sort of way. He looked at her wondering how much fun this could be.

"Yes, sweetie," she told him with a smile. "you can put some marks in it too."

He was over at her side in a second.

"So," she asked him conversationally as she held him up to reach the counter. "who's in the mood for some homemade focaccia?"

CHAPTER 14

Managing Isn't Motivating

The early morning sun shone directly into the window above the sink where Dayzie was filling the coffeemaker carafe. Her mind though was not at all on coffee or even the other tasks to get breakfast ready. She was already raring to get to Coeurs.

She pulled out her phone to look at her calendar, which showed she had an opening after the daily morning leader tour. When she checked Joanna's shared schedule, she appeared open at the same time. So she sent an appointment request for nine.

Dayzie refocused on the present, making sure her family was ready for their day, filled her purple water bottle, put her lunch in a bag, and set off to Coeurs. By the time she got to Buggy Works, Joanna had already accepted the request.

The morning leader walk revealed that another project had someone thinking about leaving the company. While Megan was thorough in sharing her updates, Dayzie noticed that she didn't spend as much time on all the risk items.

She shot Megan a knowing glance.

The morning tour ended on time, as expected, giving Dayzie enough time to race out and pick up a cup of Ethiopian brew. It wasn't for her though. Returning, she bounded into Joanna's area and pointed to the nearest open team room.

"You get this if you follow me," she announced before walking away.

Joanna, predictably, followed.

"Here you go," Dayzie said as soon as they were shut up inside the room. "I don't want you to be without your fix for this." Joanna's "thank you" was punctuated by how fast she opened the pullback sip cover, wasting no time to get her first taste.

"Okay." Her eyes were still closed in bliss. "What's up?"

Dayzie had rehearsed how to start. She had. But instead, she just blurted out, "We're doing it all wrong! We're trying to motivate folks by managing risk!"

Already enjoying her second sip, Joanna didn't lower her cup for several seconds. "Okay. I'll pretend to understand what you're talking about. But, um, what are you talking about?"

"How could you NOT know?" Dayzie's eyes danced with playful facetiousness. "You're the one with the high-sounding speech about needing to lead in this time of change."

Joanna grinned back, but still shook her head.

"Think about it." Dayzie's expression changed a little, growing more serious now. "We're focusing our energy in implementing project management and performance improvements to manage those changes. We're thinking of managing along this control perspective."

Joanna appeared to be following along so far.

"But we're not doing what you said yesterday – enabling joy in work. That's not how we're managing these changes. If we stop managing – or, better put, controlling, administering and dealing with – change and start enabling people to have joy in the change, it changes our focus."

Dayzie found herself getting animated all over again as she pulled out her tablet, revealing her version of what Megan had been scribbling. Passing it over, she said invitingly, "Take a look at this."

Joanna considered it silently while Dayzie explained its origins. And she stayed quiet for a full minute after that, taking another long sip of her coffee that seemed less about the coffee and more about her mental reflections.

Finally, she nodded. "You're onto something there. I can see Megan's math-focused thinking all over this, but this really pulls together what I was missing." Her head cocked to the side. "It's kind of scary how much this can explain. I do recall that Herzberg stuff." Another small hesitation. "Actually, now that I look at those curves, it reminds me of the Kano stuff. If my memory serves me right, I think that was built on Herzberg's ideas."

Sipping her coffee, she swallowed and tapped the page twice for emphasis. "Okay. Yes. We're not going to stop risk management or project management, I'm sure; but I think you're right that we were thinking that was all we needed to do.

We tried to lead by managing instead of leading the change and managing the risk."

"Wow! That sounded kind of cool." She stared at her coffee in playful amazement. "What's in this coffee you got me?"

Dayzie chuckled.

Joanna refocused. "We've got our work cut out for us though. That's for sure. The first thing we need to do is get the leadership team aligned on this." Her free hand flicked out in assurance. "I'll take care of that. But could you to take a hard look at how you've rolled out this project management emphasis? I think we'll see where we need to adjust our strategy given what we just talked about."

Dayzie nodded. "Consider it done!" Focaccia?"

CHAPTER 15

Learning Loop

Project metrics were not Joanna's favorite pastime. Even though she loved math, this aspect of project management seemed more like bookkeeping than analysis. And she had to work at keeping herself on task.

Dayzie had scheduled a meeting for the leadership team as promised. The earliest available time for all to meet gave Joanna two weeks to get her thoughts together. But they weren't.

Joanna found herself continually worrying about not enabling joy, or, as she processed it, letting people down. She wasn't sure if the churning in her stomach caused her headaches or the headaches caused the churning. Either way, she longed to find a way to resolve this problem and be at peace.

Providentially, right before she was at risk of spacing out again, her phone blipped with a recognizable number.

"Hi there, Pat," she answered. "How are you?"

Pat was the Program Manager at the facility outside Baltimore, which was very similar to Buggy Works. Since he knew the performance improvement initiatives would be implemented at his place next, he wanted to see how they were going over on her end so far.

"Funny you should ask," was her response, right before launching into how she was trying to figure out the best way to make sure that employee morale didn't suffer as a result.

Joanna went into details, sharing how she felt responsible for the people who'd left and the ones toying with the idea. And she explained the meeting too. It was a lot of information to take in, she knew, so she tried to lighten the conversation up a bit with a joke.

"That was kind of like drinking from a fire hydrant, wasn't it?

Pat gave a little laugh. "Yes it was, but I have an idea for you."

"I'm all ears."

"Have you looked at your latest results from the employee engagement survey data?"

That would be the data that got cranked into Coeurs' Happy Factor Index every so often, something she hadn't looked at in a while, she had to admit. "No. I'm afraid not."

"Okay." Pat sounded triumphant, as if that was the right answer to give. "Then I have a plan for you."

"Go on."

"You can take that data, and rack and stack it against your connect-create-contribute criteria. For example, the survey questions that relate to purpose, family, and mission; those are 'connect' questions."

"Hmm," she pondered out loud.

"The ones that relate to being able to do ones job, and being able to innovate on the job, are 'create' related," he mapped out. "And everything about having a sense of accomplishment, seeing jobs completed and shipped, and whether leadership is implementing their ideas? Those are very much indicative of what I think you mean by term contribute."

"Interesting," she said, grabbing a pen to start taking notes.

"Right?" He sounded pleased. "What you have here is a way to use that data to see where you're missing one or more of those elements. If you really want to practice Deming's philosophies, then you want to PDSA this."

Plan. Do. Study. Act.

Since Joanna had just been looking at the model again that morning in preparation for the meeting, the acronym spelled out in her head automatically.

PDCA or PDSA Cycle of Learning

According to Deming, management is prediction. Figuring out a process for that prediction is key to learning. Learning should be a source of joy as it makes new connections and creates new ways to create value. PDCA or PDSA are Deming's process for learning. Essentially a shorthand for the scientific method that we all learned in grade school, it stands for Plan, Do, Check (or Study) and Act. The Plan is the hypothesis the Do is the testing on a small scale, the Check or Study is exactly that and the Act is the decision to learn or start again. The term PDCA (or PDSA) has become a fairly standard acronym in many organizations.

"Make a prediction," he reiterated. "Develop a hypothesis. If folks are feeling well-connected to the value we provide customers, then they should answer yes to questions about relating to our purpose. So look to see if the results in the data support that hypothesis."

Joanna's pen kept moving.

"After you find which hypotheses hold water, you'll be smarter on where to focus your energy. My guess is that folks are feeling more distant from the 'contribute' part, what with all the project management stuff. But the process changes may be threatening their feelings too, just about their connectivity and ability to create value." He gave a little laugh. "Don't let my brilliant logic sway you here though. Go look at the data yourself."

It really did sound like the perfect answer. She couldn't wait to test it out and, if possible, develop it into something she could actually put into practice.

"Pat, that was so helpful. I think you filled in several blanks for me." She stared down at her notes. "If this works out the way we both seem to think it will, I'll owe you big time."

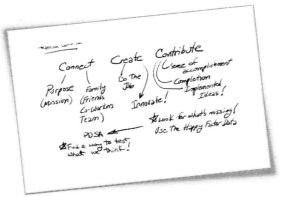

CHAPTER 16

Shop Floor Joy

Andrew popped the last gummy bear into his mouth as he strode into the machine shop.

Brandon immediately flagged him over. One of Andrew's cleverest technician artisans, Brandon began explaining how they were spending too much time making the shape they needed. He thought they might be better off using the 3D printer, which was an excellent way to build a prototype – but not usually ideal for turning out actual production items.

Backstory Note

Brandon and Andrew are discussing how to make some parts. 3D printing is a way to do that. It's essentially printing with a solid material instead of ink in, you guessed it, three dimensions. They will also talk about jigs. That's not a dance but a way to make repetitive parts by saving set-up time and ensuring uniformity.

That was especially true for such an intricate shape as the one they were talking about now. Yet Andrew listened anyway while Brandon explained his proposal.

He couldn't help but notice the man's passion on the subject, and wondered if he could apply the meeting's discussion to the situation.

His mind started to see the words that Joanna had put on the board.

Connect. Create. Contribute.

Brandon clearly had ownership of the project and a desire to improve it. He was connected to the purpose of his craft. And he was also very much about creating a better way to get it done.

It all led Andrew to a single theory, which he proceeded to play out in his head: What would happen if he suggested they not do the project or just settle for a suboptimum solution? He could easily predict the look on Brandon's face, certain it would dampen the man's desire to do a truly great job.

It was a great perspective to keep in mind. But how did he act on it? One of the things Tom had mentioned that morning was that Joanna's message was just the start. It wasn't much of a prescriptive. It was on each of them to be thinking of ways to implement it.

"So," Brandon asked. "What do you think?"

Andrew realized he'd gotten lost inside his own head and apologized. Quick to recover, he motioned Brandon to the nearest team room. "What I did catch before was very interesting, so let's go discuss this more in-depth."

Once inside, Andrew went right to the whiteboard, where he formed two columns – 3D and Fixtures – leaving a lot of space between them. Then, under each one, he made room for two more columns, this time for pros and cons.

Turning around, he pointed at the board. "Okay, let's see if we can see all the options here."

Brandon was all ready to jump in. "3D is obvious. The pros include perfect machining to plan, and rapid revision and proto-typing. Plus, it's better suited to computing complex geometry." His eyes lit up with a new thought. "If we got a printer with soluble supports, we could do some really cool stuff. Oh, and another positive would be no set up time. All we'd have to do is hit print and forget about it, so it's less machinist manpower."

Andrew put each aspect up on the board.

"The big con," Brandon admitted, "is that it's just not as accurate. The CNC machine has better tolerances. 3D can leave a bit of stair-step finish on some of the surfaces. And, weirdly, it's not perfectly repeatable."

Andrew kept writing, and Brandon kept talking.

"For small parts in particular, 3D may be quicker; but for larger parts, it becomes a toss-up. Cons are probably that we always need to make adjustments by adjusting the design, which slows things down a bit."

More Lingo Backstory

CNC stands for computer numerical control. Put simply, it's using a comput-er program to operate the machining tools. Relax. It's the conversation that mat-ters, not the technology.

Andrew nodded in agreement. "Okay, now give me your pros and cons. What's it matter to Brandon?"

His team player looked puzzled. "I think I just told you what matters, didn't I?"

Andrew nodded again. "You said what matters to the process, which was exactly what I asked. But now I want you to tell me what matters to *you*."

Still looking bewildered, Brandon played along, speaking slowly. "I like being able to rapidly improve the product, but I also like to have a slick way to put it into production. And right now, I don't think we have the best component for easy production." His hands moved with his thoughts. "I was thinking if we just cheat on efficiency a bit, we could do a lot of beta models and then see if we could find a way to minimize jigs."

Andrew contemplated that silently.

"In the old days," Brandon kept going, "a component like this would be lots of hands-on fussing. That gave folks like me a sense of ownership of design, which we appreciated. What matters to me now is having control over the artistic part while also having a guarantee on the accuracy part, a rapid ability to improve it and minimum wasted effort." He ended with his arms falling back to his sides. "But that's true for everyone."

Pondering it, Andrew took a moment before he put his own two cents in. "I think those were good answers, so here's another one: What gives you sense of ownership? 3D or the CNC machine?"

Brandon's gaze transferred to the ceiling while he weighed his answer. "I'd say it's about even."

"Okay. What gives you best accuracy control?"

"CNC."

"How about the rapid ability to improve?" Andrew was beginning to feel on a roll.

"3D."

"Minimum wasted effort?"

"3D."

Andrew nodded. "In that case, let's go with 3D. Find a way to clear one of those printers' schedules for a five day run. If you need help, go see Nico."

Looking a combination of pleased and puzzled at the whole exchange, Brandon said he would and then was out the door, presumably to take care of exactly that.

Andrew reviewed what had just happened. There were clear signs that Brandon did indeed want to connect and create. He just needed the opportunity to connect his talents to the work at hand in order to create value. And having high-speed prototyping capability maximized his creative efficiency.

That last term stopped Andrew's flow of thought. *Creative efficiency*. That would normally be something of an oxymoron. But not here.

As he played this conversation over in his mind, he saw what had really happened. As Brandon had taken ownership of the changes to the process, he had also seamlessly woven in the joy in work elements of connect, create and contribute.

The way he was seeing it right then, Joanna's little three-word idea might actually help transform their whole attitude about process improvements.

CHAPTER 17

Going All In

On her way to Buggy Works, Joanna tried to mentally rehearse how she'd run the upcoming meeting. Again, her coffee cup was sans coffee. She wanted to be patient and thorough, or at least without the stomach distress.

She continued to fret over the nagging suspicion that these ideas about joy in work would sound like just so much management gobbledygook. Would she be able to find a way to make this concept practicable?

Tom was coming down to Buggy Works specifically for the discussion, which added to the pressure. So too did the fact that it was Joanna who'd convinced him to come. She might be ready for "the next step," and she wanted to have him readily available to endorse or squash it.

Joanna arrived in the team room about five minutes early, just as she'd planned. But she wasn't the first. Brian, the finance director, was already there with his laptop open, and Andrew was lurking by the goodies table that had been set up against the far wall.

Joanna left it at a simple "hello" for both of them, seeing how they were absorbed in other tasks for the moment.

Dayzie was the next one in, followed closely by Nico, who was essentially the director of operations. Like Andrew, he was fond of fiddling with equipment, but his real talent was keeping Buggy Works humming with a steady stream of raw material coming in and a ready way to ship products out. He always said he liked to think of the company like a complex juggling act, and his job was to never let a ball hit the ground.

If anyone present was going to make Joanna nervous, it was Nico. He was a no-nonsense-approach kind of guy. He wasn't cynical per se, just not one for pretenses or buzzwords. Or chatting in general. In his world, the evidence of a good thought was a good action, which made everything in between rather superfluous.

She'd heard him say more than once that most management tools and ideas were a waste of time. So Joanna had to assume that, while Nico wouldn't be explicitly resistant, he'd be the most skeptical about using a term as squishy as "enable joy" to lead his people.

She told herself to breathe. It was going to be all right.

Once everyone was there and seated, herself included, Joanna got right to it, forgoing the niceties if for no other reason than to put Nico in a good mood.

"We've got a big opportunity here at Buggy Works," she explained. "As you all know, Tom's entrusted us to apply better processes through robust improvement strategies and to run better projects through robust project management strategies. Which automatically means that all of us need to change the way we do things."

She told herself not to look at Nico when she said that last part, her eyes flitting to the people who were already on board with her. "It's up to us. We define how well or how poorly we navigate this change. More importantly, our people need us to be clear in pointing the way. Change is when leadership is most critical."

Dayzie let out a little sound, as if to say something, but she cut herself off. Eyes darting around the room, she somewhat impishly said a demure, "Oops. Excuse me."

Catching the intent, Joanna let her last sentence hang for a moment before she proceeded.

"Anyone can manage consistency. Anyone can tell some-one to repeat a process." Her hands went out of their own ac-cord. "But when there's some change being put in place, people are going to be more attuned to what we as leaders point to, what we focus on and what we say. So this time of change is the real test of whether we're doing our jobs as leaders."

This time, she did look at Nico, for the simple reason that she didn't think she'd looked at him once so far and it was probably high time to. "For me personally, I don't think I'm doing that job well. We have several folks who have left Buggy Works, and their reasons had to do with us, not them. They didn't suddenly strike it rich and move to the Berkshires. They decided we weren't their family of choice."

Nico was watching her intently. So was the rest of the room.

"As some of you know," she resumed, "a few of us have been bouncing around an idea that we think could help us be better leaders, and interestingly enough, it's based on something right on our wall." She gestured toward the hallway. "We have that statement based on Deming that a manager's job is to enable joy in work. But apparently, we're not doing that across the board. And I think several of us have figured out why and what to do about it."

She turned to the two people who weren't in the loop. "So, Brian or Nico, I'm going to put you on the spot. What does that directive 'enable joy in work' mean to you?"

Brian was taken by surprise, and Joanna knew why. He was used to being more of a meeting spectator than a participant.

Yet he was the first one to answer. "I never really gave it much thought," he admitted, "but I figured it had to do with not being a jerk as a boss."

That got a round of appreciative laughs and grins.

Nico didn't participate in that though, which made Joanna feel like maybe she shouldn't be smiling either.

Brian, pleased with his accidental ability to lighten the mood, continued in a more serious tone. "I don't really know. I do know that Deming focused on process. He told management to stop blaming employees for what were process issues, which makes them feel more at ease doing their work, and enables them to talk about problems and how to fix them. Perhaps that helps them enjoy their day too." He added in an uncharacteristic bit of personal detail. "I know that's true for me."

Joanna stood up, non-coffee cup in hand. "That's very similar to what Dayzie, Andrew, Tom and I said a week or so ago."

Walking over to the chalkboard, she used her free hand to write out those three key words: Connect. Create. Contribute. "Until recently, I really didn't have a good working definition for Deming's advice. But now I think I have an idea on what it's all about. And thanks to Megan and Dayzie, I actually understand my own idea a bit better."

She pointed to the board. "Here it is."

Brian looked at the whiteboard with a blank stare, while Nico wrinkled his brow in thought. "Nice alliteration, Joanna. What's the point?"

Dayzie jumped in before Joanna could. "Well, we resort to dealing with these changes by" – she made air quotes with her fingers – "managing them." Her lips twisted in regret. "I think I did most of all. We have our people in this whirlwind of change so that they feel like they don't recognize their own Coeurs family anymore."

Nico steepled his fingers together and watched her. Which, as far as Joanna could tell, didn't bother Dayzie at all.

"They feel like they're outsiders," she went on, "and that they're no longer connected to what we do and how we do it. Worse yet, they're worried the new process will eliminate their personal touch and essentially turn them into robots." She was visibly trying to speak slower than her normal energetic pace to be as clear as possible. "And we have to factor in how all the new project management stuff clouded their view of the horizon; they couldn't see the endgame. In fact, we had them focusing on all the ways we might not get the project done, which is a depressing finish to emphasize, to say the least."

Nico opened his mouth, but Dayzie plowed on.

"I got it wrong. I tried to manage all these changes from control and predictability perspectives; I robbed them of their joy by failing to connect them to the new way, by failing to make sure we maximized their ability to create value, and by clouding the path for them to contribute that value."

Tom, who normally had a perfect poker face, showed a bit of amused surprise at Dayzie's passionate plea to understand. "I think I see the point. We probably all veer toward classic command-and-control management styles when the going gets uncertain. But this connect, create, and contribute directive makes for a pretty good way of evaluating where we, as leaders, may be sucking the energy out of our teams."

Joanna felt her shoulders relax just the slightest notch.

Tom wasn't done quite yet though. "What I'm wondering now is whether we can also figure out how to make it tell us what we need to do; not just show us how we missed the boat."

Nico got a word in then. "I agree. This is good in one sense, but I don't see how it helps me on a typical day"

Joanna's shoulders went right back to stiff again. This was the point she figured they'd get stuck at.

Fortunately, Andrew chimed in before she could get herself too worked up. "I actually do see a way this could help me at least. When we eliminate some tasks or make a jig that eliminates the need for artisan precision, I need to make sure we don't throw the baby out with the bathwater." He gestured over at her. "Or, to use Joanna's terms, to throw 'connect' and 'create' out with the process waste."

Nico looked at Andrew with relative amusement. "Yeah. Have fun figuring that out."

Joanna decided it was time to take control of the conversation again. "I think I have a way for us to develop a prescriptive by first using Dayzie's diagnostic."

She sketched out a set of curves on the whiteboard. "What we have here is some artwork cooked up by Megan and Dayzie; a picture of what Deming might have meant by all this stuff. This mashes together Herzberg's motivation theory with the Kano model."

Pointing out each necessary element, she explained out the bottom curve, which represented pay, benefits, nice offices and other such physiological stuff. Safety, security, and sustenance: the dissatisfiers.

Brian spoke up. "What are those axes?"

Joanna blinked. "Oh right. Yes. It's basically dissatisfaction below the horizontal line, and motivators above it. I think Kano called it delight.'"

She partially erased the word "Motivators" and scrawled in "Joy" in its place. "And then we have this upper curve. This is where we have our 'connect, create, and contribute.' What it tells us is that when we get it wrong, we slide down the curve and lose joy." She could hear her own voice getting more passionate. "What we need to figure out is how to climb it. How to enable joy or, more specifically, how to enable the ability to connect, create, and contribute."

And here came her big reveal. She took a deep breath in through her nose and then let it out. "What I think we can do is plot what we do as leaders on this graphic, and see what we do that enables joy."

"Real quick." Brian, ever attentive to details, moved his finger side to side. "What's the horizontal axis represent?"

Dayzie jumped in, allowing Joanna to pick up her cup once again. "It has something to do with time." Dayzie's arms signaled clear directions to the left and then to the right. "Like, here's where we were. And here's where we're going."

So much for that sip. Joanna put her cup back down as she thought of a better way of describing it. "Let's try this: To the left of the vertical line is stuff we do that's reactive; and to the right is stuff we do that's proactive."

Everyone waited.

She obliged. "If someone doesn't have enough pay or benefits, we can fix that. We react to that situation, and they get this rapid rise because their three S's are satisfied."

Tom leaned back a little in his chair. Nico had a pointed finger on one cheek. And Dayzie looked like she wanted to start cheering Joanna on with something motivational.

Joanna made sure not to let the visual distract her, even if it was a little amusing. "If we keep folks connected and keep their ability to create value and contribute it open as well, then we have a way to unleash an increase in joy, which should spike our productivity too."

She wrinkled her nose. Maybe she needed that cheer after all.

"I'm sorry if I made this confusing, but if we think of it this way, we may get some insight. If we're reacting, it's on the left. If we're pro-acting, as it were, it's on the right."

Andrew got up, stopping at the catering table to pop a strawberry in his mouth on his way to the board – which he wasn't done chewing before he started speaking. "I kind of get it. When we do Six Sigma stuff, we're preventing problems. So it's proactive, but it's not a delighter. We're just getting rid of problems."

He swallowed, then went right back to summarizing. "It gets rid of the headache, sure, but lack of a headache isn't a source of joy. So a Six Sigma event would be on the right on the lower curve."

He then made an arc with his hand on the upper section of the graph. "But when we do a Lean event, we usually create entirely new process capabilities, and that could be on this upper curve." He spared a glance to his left. "Am I seeing it right, Joanna?"

She smiled. "Yes! And you're explaining it great too."

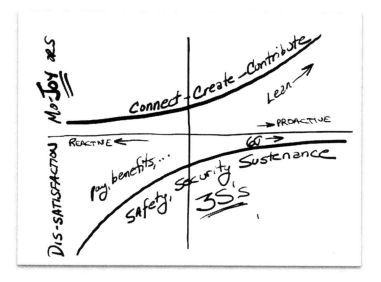

Tom leaned forward again. "I think we should look into this further."

That got an instantaneous smirk from the rest of the group, since they all knew he was the consummate researcher. He wouldn't buy a pair of socks without first doing a thorough Internet search on them.

Tom rolled his eyes in good-natured acceptance. "Yes, I know. But I'm specifically talking about a beta test."

Everyone stopped smirking and started listening.

"For example," he said, "say you sketch out a template, and we tell folks to put it on their notepad or whatever portable device they use. Then they fill them out during the planning meetings or just after." He spread out his hands. "We could overlay the results and get a Buggy Works picture of how well we're living up to our joy philosophy. And more importantly, if this works like you've explained, then we'll also get a forward-looking predictor of potential employee engagement issues."

Joanna let out a thoughtful little, "Hmm."

"Let's see what happens," Tom added. "But to show I'm all in, I'll even track my own actions. So let me know when you get a template." He smiled. "Who knows? This just might be crazy enough to work."

His words were encouraging, yes, but they didn't exactly alleviate the healthy dose of anxiety Joanna felt, and something told her that Dayzie was on the same page as her. Neither of them wanted to needlessly cycle the leadership team on some random thought experiment. More importantly, they truly wanted to get to the root of the issue of why employees were becoming disenchanted at Coeurs.

Joanna noticed how Nico took a deep breath when Tom was done, and she didn't need to ask him about it in order to interpret the signal. He would have a 'wait and see' approach. That was a given.

For his part, Brian looked interested enough, but he clearly didn't look like he thought any of it affected his work.

Neither man's reaction was a good sign in Joanna's nervous book.

Andrew, however, caught her eye with eyebrows raised in friendly challenge. "Alright then," he said, "let's go do this."

CHAPTER 18

Unexpected Places for Joy

M egan sat in a meeting room with Dayzie across from her, both of them poring over the details of the project. So far, it appeared that cost and schedule were barely in the green and were trending poorly. One little bump in the road, and they'd be preparing a statement for the board explaining why they'd failed.

Megan pulled out the risk register, wondering if there were some hazards they may have overlooked or missed. But before she could suggest any such thing, the conversation from Joanna's meeting played out in her mind.

"How would you go about using that connect, create and contribute philosophy for this situation?" She asked. "The way I see it, we have a project underway with a project team full of well-defined roles and responsibilities that should be connected to why we need to do this well." She frowned. "This project is all about creating the design, prototype and manufacturing process for our keystone product. Plus, we're all working to make it a reality, and the whole project management approach should be helping us realize that this really will contribute value to the customer and the company."

Megan let out a sigh. "So why are people getting frustrated when it seems like we've got all three angles covered?"

Pushing her tablet out of the way, Dayzie took a long sip from her purple water bottle first. "I completely agree. But let's take a look at how the team may see some of our project management tools. When they see this huge risk register, what do you think it tells them?"

Megan waved that away. "Like I said earlier, it makes them focus on how we might not get it done."

"Yes," Dayzie agreed. "But it may also be sending the unintended message that we're only concerned about cost and schedule. We lose the excitement part about our new product."

"Ooh!" Megan's eyes lit up. "That's good. That's really good. Creating and contributing are exciting factors, and risk management steers us away from that kind of emotion."

A new thought hit her though, which had her mood crashing right back down. "Then again, let's face it: We can't go willy-nilly ignoring the risks. We owe it to our customers and our company to be good stewards."

Dayzie winced at the logic but promptly thumped her bottle down on the table. "We can't be stuck with thinking that it has to be one *or* the other." She heavily emphasized the word or.

Startled, Megan tried to register what she'd just said even while she waited for more. But after a few expectant seconds of analyzing Dayzie's expression, she realized there wasn't going to be more. She was trying to motivate Megan into coming up with the answer herself.

With some tired reluctance, Megan decided to play along, just with an added touch of stalling. "I think I know what you're referring to. That 'or versus and' stuff comes up in several leadership and change workshops. Regardless, what you're trying to get me to think of is how we can have both the risk assessment and the excitement."

Dayzie kept the energy going, seamlessly picking up where Megan had left off. "That means that somehow, we have to have both risk management and project excitement in a sort of creative tension. My gut instinct is that this is what Joanna meant about differentiating between leading people and managing work." She drummed her fingers against her water bottle. "We need to keep the risk stuff focused on the facts – the predictions, the schedule, the cost; everything that exists on paper. If we only keep that at the center of our project conversations, then we will hide the joy aspects. But, by using that connect, create and contribute template, we should be able to keep joy in the conversation while not just adding a bunch of mumbo-jumbo, kumbaya stuff." Another subtle drum roll of her fingers. "I'm thinking a question that allows us to interrogate joy as much as we interrogate project risks will make all the difference.

Megan took her time responding. "You know that new ISO recertification we're planning? That's yet another change we're going to be foisting on folks."

"Yeah," Dayzie said, losing some of her enthusiasm. "I completely forgot about that."

Megan held up a hand in reassurance. "I was actually rather excited because risk management gets a bigger emphasis in the new version. I thought that was a good validation of what we're doing and also a nice selling point to the board on why the resources we're spending are being well used."

"I'm still waiting for you to make me feel better," Dayzie pointed out.

"Don't worry," Megan promised. "It's just that I'm now having a bit of a revelation. Sections four through six don't just talk about risk management. They describe both risk *and* opportunity." She could feel her eyes light up. "I think that needs to be our approach. I mean, the way I'm seeing it right now, addressing both risks and opportunities are actually two sides of the same coin."

ISO: Quick Note
ISO is an abbreviation for a system of certifications that organizations can attain to attest to their compliance with certain quality standards recognized worldwide. In this fable, they are referring to ISO 9001:2015, a revised version that now has provisions for risk management and knowledge management. The cool takeaway is how Connect, Create, Contribute play a role in helping businesses achieve success per industry standards.

"I see where you're going, but hold up one second." Dayzie started fiddling with her tablet, entering in search data and then thumbing through whatever results had popped up.

Judging by her response, it must have been some pretty good data.

"That's the answer to our riddle!" Dayzie gasped. "It's right there in the boring ISO stuff! Who'd have guessed it!"

Megan's eyebrows both rose, waiting for her colleague to elaborate. And this time, she'd better, because Megan had no clue what she was talking about.

Dayzie took a breath. "We need to take our risk stuff and revamp it. Yes, I know it's a ton of work; and yes, I know our folks will have a fit. But maybe we – yes, you and me – can start weaving…" She paused. "I can't believe I'm going to say this, but, start weaving joy into our risk conversations."

Dayzie's eyes were seemingly searching the air for what to say next, and Megan wondered if she was fast becoming a spectator to this conversation.

"I guess this is actually pretty similar to what I was thinking at the start. But with a new twist, and that is being what we need to have documented proof of for recertification. Having that joy part in project conversations isn't just a feel-good exercise. It has" – Dayzie paused, her face scrunching to find the right word – "Darn! You know what I mean."

Surprisingly, Megan actually did think she was starting to follow along. Though that didn't mean she was ready to fill in the blanks just yet.

Dayzie didn't seem to notice her hesitancy anyway. She was still searching for the right term.

"Business value?" She wondered aloud. "No, uh – business sense! It makes business sense, not just people sense. In any case, we'll figure out how to say it. The point is that now this joy in work stuff, all this connect, create and contribute, has a way to be put in place, and a way to package it for Tom to take to the board as an satisfying an actual business need."

Megan could feel her smile turn up. She began to feel a bit of relief, and yet, at the same time, she wasn't complete sure she'd understood everything that Dayzie had excitedly talked about. She stood up and tapped her tablet on the table. Looking at Dayzie, she softly stated, "If you're saying what I think you're saying, then I completely agree that we've got a business answer to this joy in work stuff. Although, quite honestly, I'm not sure we haven't gotten a little crazy here and tomorrow none of this will make sense to me. You can count on me to keep thinking this over until I'm comfortable."

CHAPTER 19

Wrenching Joy

Nico was lying on the cold garage floor having an unspoken conversation with an inanimate object. He was struggling with a rusted bolt that refused to give in to his tapping, banging, mentally-projected verbal abuse, and even generous dosages of Liquid Wrench.

He had planned to tear apart the clutch on his bride's Mini Cooper, it being the weekend and all. She was at an all-day women-in-ministry conference, so he'd figured it was the perfect time to be elbow deep in grease.

Nico's hobbies were all about working with his hands in precision work. When he did carpentry, it was all about perfect miter cuts and flawless polyurethane finishes. When he did electrical work, it was all about careful circuit loading and neatly bundled connection boxes. And when he worked on the Cooper, it was all about a passion to make it just a little bit better than its German engineers had.

In his typical fastidious fashion, Nico had meticulously laid out his tarps on the garage floor. He'd driven the car up onto ramp jacks and securely blocked the wheels. A cool morning, the overhead door was open for both light and fresh air.

Clutch replacement on a Mini was a task that would intimidate most amateur mechanics. It required removing the bumper, the axles and the transmission – hardly a job for the fainthearted.

It probably didn't help that he was so distracted, struggling to see the value of this connect, create, contribute mantra the leadership team was rallying around. It wasn't that he thought it a bad idea. He respected their efforts and wanted to see how it might play out. It was just that he couldn't wrap his head around it right now.

And that was bothering him about as much as the repair to the Cooper was.

For all practical purposes, he was the consummate operations director, so he needed to be on board if they were going to start implementing some company-wide actionable mindset. And he'd much rather it be something he understood.

Then again, it was true that someone had to do something. The reality was that folks were leaving Coeurs, and that didn't make anyone's job easier.

He gave the bolt another attempted turn, but still nothing. Which was frustrating, to say the least.

Normally, Nico had a can-do attitude that was open to learning from mistakes. But the situation above him didn't seem to be lending itself to a teaching moment. All he could sense was frustration at a delay in his progress.

He'd thought through the whole process beforehand too, trying to consider every angle he possible could. He'd already downloaded several videos and instructions and blogs, positioning his laptop open and angled next to him so that he could easily see the screen. That way, he was ready for any circumstance.

Or so he'd thought.

As the morning turned to midday, Nico was finding that his self-appointed task was testing both his patience and his mechanic skills. If it wasn't a stubborn axle nut, it was transmission oil that seemed to drain with a mind of its own, not only into his catch pan but also onto the garage floor, setting him ever further back. Several times, he just stared at the entire undercarriage and wondered if maybe this should have been a job for an actual mechanic.

After fighting the Torx bolts that were stubbornly holding the pressure plate to the flywheel, Nico noticed that he was now ready to answer a stomach that was growling for lunch. Cleaning himself up as best as he could, he gingerly slid on his socks into the kitchen, careful to keep his now-greasy clothes from touching the cabinets. He used the same kind of caution as he popped a frozen beef dinner into the microwave and then checked out the refrigerator with a contemplative air. He usually only had water with lunch, but there was a bottle of homemade brew sitting there from the last time his brother was over. Perhaps a little fermented grain would give him additional patience with what was becoming an aggravating experience.

Why, Nico wondered, was he still looking forward to doing this when it was so far just one giant series of setbacks and frustrations? Yet there he was, refusing to give up. And not just for the hopeful satisfaction of getting it done, but the actual process of doing it. At first, second and third consideration, it made no sense.

What if, the fourth time around, he analyzed it through Joanna's intrinsic motivators?

Connect. Create. Contribute.

With that new idea settling over him, Nico's scientific mind went right to setting up the hypothesis. If the theory was solid, it would explain why he'd decided to spend a perfectly wonderful Saturday afternoon lying on a garage floor, fighting stubborn bolts and cleaning up misbehaved transmission oil.

He popped off the bottle top.

On the surface, fixing the Mini this time was hard work, not to mention technologically unforgiving; physically difficult with its crazy, cramped spaces; and pretty risky, with the possibility of really messing up constantly hovering over his head.

Nico knew his wife loved her Mini. He personally had a preference for classic American muscle, but knowing her preference was slightly different, he had bought her the little car – and hadn't regretted it since. The vehicle had become their escape machine, and they had many memories associated with it.

Whenever it had an issue, Nico was usually more than happy to take on the task. That included modifying various body features using the body repair and welding techniques he'd taught himself along the way.

In short, this wasn't just a Mini. It was their Mini, to the point where it even had a spot in their Christmas card photo.

Nico felt connected to it.

Connected.

He took a long sip of his brother's brew, then immediately winced. "Whoa, brother; a little heavy on the hops there."

Grabbing his microwave meal next, he settled himself on the back porch where grease wouldn't be such an issue. Plus, it was a beautiful day and a little fresh air couldn't hurt.

It didn't, as his mind went right back to the philosophical puzzle, and whether it could be translated into something more practical.

He took a bite of meat and potatoes, chewing thoughtfully. "We're connected to the car because it's kind of our identity, part of our treasured memories. Maybe that's the reason I don't send it to the shop and do this work myself."

The next term, then, was create. Which seemed simplistic enough. Of course he liked to create stuff but today's Mini challenge was all about fixing.

Mindlessly he sipped down some beer. The hoppiness made it a more conscious act.

"Fixing is sort of like creating," he thought. "Ok, I can make sense of that. And doesn't everyone like that?"

It struck him while he was going for another bite that he was simply verifying Joanna's point. For him personally, if his wife had decided to surprise him by sending the Mini off to the shop, he would have been a bit bummed. This didn't seem logical. Why would he have been bummed? He knew the answer. Because someone else would have created the fix, or, as he started to see it now, someone else would have had the joy in work.

He sat back in his deck chair and took a swig. It seemed to be an acquired taste, because the hoppiness didn't seem so obnoxious anymore. Maybe his brother's creation was better than he first judged after all.

Rather the same with Joanna's idea.

Her last term: contribute. He needed to think about that one some more though. And the Mini comparison did seem to be helping.

When it was all said and done, he wanted to have a car that was useful, of course. He didn't really just tinker around with cars for the tinkering, though there was definitely joy in the effort. He did it because he could make it better. And because, in some way, he was continually improving the gift to his wife.

By way of comparison, he contemplated what his attitude would be like if he had to jump through all sorts of permits and paperwork in the car-fixing process. If that were the case, he'd probably pay a mechanic to do it. "Well, I'll be darned," he muttered to himself.

The whole thing was making sense. Despite the difficulties before him and behind him, he enjoyed the work he'd set out to do. Maybe it was fun, but even when it wasn't, he got a genuine sense of enjoyment from doing it.

Connect. Create. Contribute.

Keep the joy in work.

He scooped up the last remnants of gravy on his tray and even downed the sediment from the bottle of the bottle.

I can work with that.

He stretched his back and legs as he got out of his chair. It was time to get back to work. There was joy to be had, even while fighting a stubborn shaft seal.

CHAPTER 20

Contemplative Joy

The knot in her stomach felt as uncomfortable as ever. Joanna found she was still wrestling with her decision to be away from Coeurs at this critical time. There had been many times in her past when she had cancelled vacations to please her boss. But she knew she had to pull some serious thoughts together now – for herself.

She looked down at the pile of hiking, camping, and journaling paraphernalia on the floor. To some, it may have looked like a mess, but Joanna was fully cognizant of every single item there.

For the past several years, she had made an annual habit of disappearing for a little more than a week. She purposely chose autumn to ensure that she'd be out of the normal tourist months but before the hunting season. While she would prefer warmer nights, the solitude was worth the evening chill.

No company. No expectations. No pressure. That was what she needed.

Joanna tried to envision the joy of the upcoming trip: a few days of camping preceded by a few quiet days at a monastery hidden in the beautiful, tree-covered hills. The monastery's property didn't even get cell reception, which was exactly to her liking.

It was one of the few times she could just stop and really think. Really breathe.

She arrived at the monastery and quickly re-appreciated the rich fulfillment of the sisters living there: how their daily rhythm – a rhythm dating back to the Dark Ages – was driven first and foremost by their core values instead of the deluge of distractions out in the regular world. They had a never-ending priority to be in constant communion, awareness and relationship with God.

Wow, she thought. *These folks have never heard of Deming, but they're certainly all about enabling joy in work.*

And what a beautiful work it was being in deep connection with the purpose of their prayers and the people of their prayers and the fellowship of their praying community. Connecting was their first and most clearly evident foundation for joy.

As Joanna went about the routine of the monastery schedule, she was also seeking to see whether the sisters also created. Sure, there were some monastery products, but those were only to provide sustenance. To pay the bills. Probably not the creations that were their deep source of enabling joy.

Then she saw it. What this community created was a deeper connection between the eternal and temporal; between the all-loving and the needing to be loved; between the search for joy and the source of joy.

And they didn't just do it for the joy of doing it, but also for the joy it brought others. Yes, they loved their work of prayer; but that prayer had a purpose – a contributory value to rhythm and the kind of real relationship that could be forged between a people and their Creator.

For the first time, Joanna found herself recognizing the completeness of this very ancient tradition and its deep reflection of joy in work.

After a couple of days that only seemed to be hours, Joanna gave warm goodbyes to the sisters and set out for the second half of her vacation: several days of hiking, wildlife watching, insect photo-taking, and camping. Out there, she would be even more alone, and so she carefully checked her gear and supplies before she set out. She had requested permission to hike and sleep in the area's game lands nearby, so she also checked to make sure she had the printed email confirmation from the property's owners.

Hiking several miles to the small glade she had previously scouted out on Google Earth, she found it to be as beautiful as envisioned. Near a quick-flowing stream, she figured that its location on the southern face and between the mountains should allow for maximum sun.

Joanna got out her phone. "Oh rats," she said aloud as she saw "No Service" across the top of the screen. She had seen a cell tower on a nearby hill and assumed her location would be in service, but clearly that wasn't the case.

Torn on what to do, she took a deep breath.

"I'm hungry and ready to settle. I don't really have the daylight left to find another spot," she mumbled to herself.

Part of the agreement to stay on the game lands was to stay in cell range for any emergency, a promise she had also made to her brothers, who thought she was being a bit too risky camping out alone in an area frequented by bears, coyotes, and even mountain lions. In some ways, their concern annoyed her. She pretended it was because she didn't like to admit a reliance on modern technology, but really it was because she liked to think she could do it on her own. On her own, there was no risk of failing to please someone else.

Joanna started wandering around, holding her phone at arms length as if that would make a difference in getting a signal. She was doing it half-heartedly and had almost talked herself out of keeping her promise altogether. Just as she was getting her dander up thinking, *I'm just fine on my own*, she was startled out her reverie by a distinct thump and tug at her shoe.

CHAPTER 21

Speed Bump

Tom shook his head as he ended the call. It hadn't been a complete nightmare, but it hadn't gone great either.

The whole time, he was very well aware that the board was going to want answers to its challenge, and very soon. Thanks to Mr. Ellis.

Ellis was a particularly irascible member of the board who held a lot of sway, almost by intimidation, over many of the other members. The man wasn't nearly as accomplished or educated as the rest of the board, though he did provide value through a particularly down-to-earth reality check, which he brought to the meetings. That would have been a great contribution all by itself, but his impatience and need for instant proof eroded the group's ability to work toward common ground. And while nobody really respected his pugnacious approach, they still allowed him to run roughshod over meetings out of sheer exhaustion, if nothing else.

Through Tom's entire time as CEO of Coeurs, Ellis had been a thorn in his side. His move to a less hierarchical structure and his style as a subtly serving leader were alien concepts to Ellis, who had succeeded just fine as a bully boss for over thirty years.

That fact had been on full display during the conference call.

Now, Ellis' tantrum-like theatrics and incessant nagging had the rest of the board also growing impatient to get answers and see results to their challenges. Tom did think that Ellis had managed to influence some of them but, as usual, some of them were simply willing to throw anyone else to the wolves if it could just mean Ellis would be quiet already.

Tom couldn't entirely blame them for that mindset. The old curmudgeon had made him antsy too.

If I only had something tangible to report.

Then he had to rethink that statement.

Something tangible and Ellis-approvable.

He felt a bit of envy, maybe anger, that Joanna had opted to keep her vacation plans and disappear at this critical time. Tom still felt somewhat uncomfortable with the ideas that Joanna and the leadership team had developed. It wasn't that the ideas didn't sound promising. If it were all up to him, he might even be able to get behind them all the way. As it was, he still found them a fundamentally sound potential approach. But he also saw that it might seem too trivial.

Too often, executive teams and boards preferred the heavy-hitting approaches of reorganizations, the meticulous approach of Six Sigma, or the promise of a new culture that so many consulting firms were overly eager to help them achieve.

This approach was none of that. It was, at its core, an introspective philosophy that required leaders to assess themselves on a seemingly simple question: Were they enabling joy in work?

Deming's work had stood the test of time, with over 30 years proving that it wasn't a flavor of the month. Sure, many organizations had treated it as such, but the sound principles remained.

Yet Tom still wasn't looking forward to convincing Mr. Ellis. He was even beginning to think his agreement with Joanna and the other team leaders had been premature. He was going to need some sort of concrete conviction that this was indeed the key to implementing the board's ideas.

And he needed it fast.

CHAPTER 22

Serpent

"What in the world!" Joanna gasped, looking down to see the unmistakable triangular shape of a copperhead snake recoiling from its strike. A small one, it seemed pretty upset by their encounter and quickly stole away.

Watching it in utter shock, Joanna felt her heart rate accelerate a bit more before it started declining back to something normal.

In her inattentive wandering to find reception, she'd been less observant of the ground below. She'd been stepping onto and over rocks without acknowledging that, on this southern face, they would be warm: perfect lounging pads for certain common denizens of the Berkshire Mountains.

Even though she didn't feel any pain or rushing venom, Joanna studied her boot, which now featured two neat holes in the thick heel.

Unbelievable. Praise God for big favors!

Her mind raced with thoughts ranging from the sublime to the ridiculous, including words from that Genesis account she'd built so much on already. Chapter three. Verse fifteen, she told herself by rote.

> *I will put enmity between you and the woman,*
> *and between your offspring and hers; They will strike*
> *at your head, while you strike at their heel."*

And somewhere behind that were the ridiculous questions of whether the holes could be repaired for free or possibly used as a marketing story.

Those only took up the smallest fractions of her mind though. Joanna was mostly focused on the sublime, with one reflection leading to another down a path of realizations.

She could now see how her seemingly noble intention to "do it on her own" was not really just about her constant efforts to please others. It was hauntingly similar to Adam and Eve's choice to do it on their own. In resisting her brothers' advice to stay in cell range, she had turned away a gift of love that she'd mistaken as a restriction of her independence. She realized that, in many ways, she was doing this at Coeurs too, where she was constantly thinking she had to handle everything herself.

Untying and pulling off her boot, she double-checked that her foot was indeed safe from harm. While she was relieved to see no mark on her foot, her heart and mind still wrestled with the thoughts that this reptile encounter had triggered.

How can I accept that connect is a two-way street?

CHAPTER 23

Life Changer

Even though the autumn afternoon was cool and overcast, Andrew was in a full sweat after running 5k. He had left work quickly to enjoy an outdoor workout.

Now, he was cycling back home like a yellow jersey was on the line. But as much as his body was burning calories, his mind may have been burning more.

There was just a lot to think about.

Andrew typically spent a portion of his weekends and many of his nights as a high school wrestling coach, earning the young athletes' respect in more than slide-bys and merkels. He had also made a point of showing them how to take what they learned on the mat during all those hours of grueling training, and apply those lessons to life.

After graduating the program, many of the athletes still stayed in touch, giving him a chance to continue mentoring them along the way.

For many of the issues that came up, Andrew found it fairly easy to help them through sports analogies. They often broke down to; hard work, dedication, focus on a goal, gain through pain, one-percent inspiration, ninety-nine-percent perspiration, or other such terms. Those all worked well more often than not, but the one situation he struggled to apply them to was the puzzling dilemma known as "failure to launch."

He'd found that a number of his mentees – or their girl-friends – had an issue wherein they couldn't bring themselves to leave home and support themselves, or make a real commitment to a significant other and start their own lives.

Rick, the younger man he'd run with this afternoon, was one such individual. Talented, sociable, intelligent, and healthy, it was puzzling why this twenty-nine year-old was so content to still live with his parents. Having coached him in wrestling, Andrew had seen many situations that proved Rick had drive and motivation. When he wanted.

That was what he was puzzling over now while he rode his bike home from the race. What was keeping the man from unleashing his potential, purpose, and passion?

Joanna's crazy sketch of the mother changing a diaper made a strange appearance in his head, which led Andrew to start thinking about his niece. A bounding bundle of one-year-old energy, she had just mastered the art of walking, and her vocabulary was increasing by several words a day.

He had recently heard how those were the two biggest changes in a person's life and the two most difficult skills to learn: to walk and to talk. They were life skills that dramatically changed babies' worlds, yet they learned them so willingly and joyfully.

Joy in learning. Joy in change.

Andrew came to the last long incline. He gradually down-shifted while trying to maintain speed. Always competitive, he had run pretty hard to keep a competitive pace with his mentee. So his legs were now begging for a respite.

But Andrew refused to grant them that, hoping that his thoughts would keep him from dwelling too hard on the grow-ing discomfort in his calf muscles.

Rick needed a big change: to move out on his own, make a commitment to his girlfriend, and decide to really support him-self already. But he wasn't. Instead, he had opted to value com-fort: safety, security, and Mom's home cooking. Apparently, he was blind to the joy that connecting to a life purpose, creating value to that purpose and contributing something from it would provide.

It was a good summation, and Andrew found that he now knew the type of coach he needed to be for Rick. He had to en-able joy. He had to help Rick realize that life wasn't just about surviving or even merely enjoying the present, but also about finding joy in a changing future – joy in changing the present into the future.

His calves burning in pain, Andrew sat up in his bike seat as his wheels crested the soft apex of the hill. From there, he stopped pedaling altogether, letting his bike coast effortlessly on the slight descent that came right before the home stretch. The late morning air blowing through his sweaty shirt provided a welcome evaporative cooling effect. And he felt like his mind was just as rewarded.

Andrew was nothing short of exuberant. Not only had he solved the equation for how to coach Rick, but also had just figured out how to help his team at Coeurs.

CHAPTER 24

More Mystery

Dayzie highlighted an entire screen's worth of emails, then hit the delete button.

"EEK!"

The sense of mailbox cleaning satisfaction was laced with a bit of dread as hundred of bytes got shuttled to the trashcan, especially since she was doing this to Joanna's email.

Dayzie liked covering for Joanna while she was away on vacation, a role she took very seriously from start to finish. She wanted to be able to give Joanna an empty inbox when she returned considering how there were few things that killed a vacation mood faster than seeing a bazillion emails waiting to be resolved.

That task accomplished for the time being, Dayzie moved reluctantly on to overseeing the morning walk. If it was up to her, she might have stopped midway through the week because the news she was getting continued to be on the troubling side.

There were still grumblings and mumblings of folks looking to leave Coeurs.

And now we'll have to explain why the Happy Factor Index has slipped, she thought to herself, reflecting on the report she'd seen in Joanna's mailbox.

A key data point in that catalog was one that measured how long it took for people to respond to others' requests for help. By coding request-oriented emails similar to a job ticket, Coeurs was able to track the response time for supporting one another. A dip in this statistic was considered a forewarning of productivity decline, but more critically, of morale decline. This commonly understood chain of events triggered a thought for Dayzie.

When folks don't connect, create and contribute to each other, there can't be joy.

What am I doing wrong?

With the morning tour concluded, Dayzie tugged on Megan's arm.

"What in the world is going on?" she asked, her voice low but passionate. "You and I are pretty nice people and pretty darn competent. Yet we pour our hearts and minds into this effort only to find ourselves on the brink of disaster!"

Megan grimaced. "I know. I'm afraid Joanna's going to come back and get a cold splash of reality after her disappearing-act vacation. And frankly, I'm not feeling too good about how well I'm preventing any of this from happening."

Dayzie's voice lost a lot of its frustration to take on a telling sadness instead. "I'm afraid all that stuff we were talking about with joy in work is just that: talk."

"Maybe so." Megan appeared thoughtful. "But I've been thinking about it, and I'm starting to see something mathematical in what we talked about before."

Dayzie shot her a quizzical glance.

"I might have a way to work this out," Megan added with cautious optimism.

That last sentence transformed Dayzie's concerned expression into a curious grin. "Megan, you are a most confusing nerd. Math based joy; I can't wait to see you pull out the algebra on this one."

CHAPTER 25

Cloudy Clarity

The full moon was peering through the clouds and into the clearing where Joanna was putting her boot back on. It was now after dusk, but being remote from urban light pollution allowed even just that fraction of light to provide her with the ability to put together her shelter for the evening. Because as much as she wanted to contemplate her revelation from Scripture, she needed to take care of first things first.

Shelter, security, and sustenance.

Joanna pitched her tent on a smooth bedding of pine needles, breathing in the scent as she did. Her one-person tent, a veteran of many camping adventures, was now like a good friend.

"Okay, no other people around, but I'm not really alone," she mumbled to herself as she strung her aluminum mess kit on a line so as to fashion a noisemaker for other forest friends.

At that moment, sustenance was the least of her concerns. She had all the proteins, carbs, and water she needed. This meant she was now ready for some spiritual and emotional nourishment, so she zipped the tent closed and pulled herself into her sleeping bag. The snake episode had drained her more than she wanted to admit, and she needed something else to focus on. That's why she put on her headlamp and pulled out the book she'd brought, which, coincidentally, was about relationships: staying connected.

Rain started to hit the tent.

She wasn't in cell range, of course, which had felt rather freeing at first. Now though, Joanna was acutely aware of how she'd been denying that connection was a component of joy.

There was a faint sound outside: her utensils tinkling on the line, which made her feel even smaller in the moment. The rain made it hard to figure out if it was just the wind, yet she had thought she'd bundled her utensils too heavily to turn into a wind chime.

She listened harder, her imagination wanting to project a hundred different growls, howls and snorts into the sounds of the rain in the foliage and the gurgling of newly created rivulets.

Her thoughts raced.

Why in the world did I get out of cell range?

Did I leave food out there?

She toyed with whether she should peek out or just stay still, straining to determine any change in the noises.

Joanna really, really wanted a cell signal now, coming to the definite determination that she didn't need to prove she was some kind of Grizzly Adams. She didn't even know who this

Grizzly Adams was nor why that name had popped in her head. But now, an image of a bear played in her mind. While she had always wanted to see a bear, she would prefer doing so during daylight hours and with some significant distance between them.

Her heart was still pounding, but now she was pretty sure the only remaining noise was the steady rain. Whether the whole thing had been a product of her imagination or not was still up in the air, but she was now wide awake. Awake and feeling very alone.

Seeking a distraction, she reflected on her approach to her work at Coeurs. She always favored the idea of doing it all by herself, even though as a project team leader, she knew that no project could succeed with only one person. She contrasted that thought with how she assumed that her role as the nominal program manager was a solitary assignment. Now she was seeing that maybe being connected was a necessity to better create value even in this seemingly non-team role. She didn't need to singularly shoulder that burden; she needed to have more trust. There was no reason for her not to.

Connect. We are community.

It was a critical part of creating value and the subtle beauty of the creation story.

Let us create man.

Her brothers wanted her to stay connected because they cared. They could only serve – could only create value – when and if they stayed connected.

The rain beat harder on the tent, with droplets working their way down the seams.

Okay. Just hold tight for a few more hours.

In the meantime, she supposed she would simply have to connect to the only One she could right then.

CHAPTER 26

Off the Sofa

Andrew finished his ride with a sprint, which he very quickly regretted. His competitive spirit could take him far, but it had a bad habit of taking him too far at times. He was trying to figure out is his stomach was rebelling or just empty. He decided to believe the latter.

Inside, at his refrigerator, Andrew gazed at his options, ultimately grabbing a yogurt, cheese, eggs and milk, with a last-second grab for the orange juice as well.

As a frying pan hit the stove and the yogurt surrendered its top, Andrew thought back to a sign on the coach's office in his high school wrestling room.

> "We are what we repeatedly do. Excellence is not an act, but a habit." — Aristotle

Both with Rick and at work, people were expecting an act of excellence instantaneously, when they actually had to practice it. Repeatedly. That was his ah-ha moment: the key he was searching for. It was a way to help himself and his Coeurs compatriots get their logical heads around the seemingly gooey concept of enabling joy in work.

But just to make sure it could work, he decided to test his thinking out on his mentee before he brought it to the big leagues. First though, he threw a dash of oil into the frying pan, and then some garlic on top of that. Then he put his phone on speaker and called up his mentee.

A groggy voice mumbled "hey" on the other end, as if their run hadn't ever happened.

Slightly baffled and maybe even a little annoyed, Andrew told himself not to get derailed. "Hey Rick, what are you up to?"

"Not much," Rick admitted without a twinge of guilt. "Just killing time playing *Halo* until I see what the rest of the guys are doing tonight. Why?"

Andrew just went for it. "Why in wrestling practice do you think we're always doing drills, even the ones we all hate like the spin?"

"Huh?" Rick sounded confused. Or distracted. "What?"

"Why do we do those drills?" Andrew pressed.

His responding shrug was almost audible. "Conditioning, I guess."

"Conditioning what?"

"Our fitness. No," he corrected himself, sounding like he might actually be focused now. "Like our shape. You know – conditioning to stay in shape."

"Then why don't we just only run laps or do hot yoga?" Andrew pressed further.

For whatever reason, that took a second to process on the other end. "Because we're not runners or yoga - uh - doers?"

"Right." *Or at least, close enough.* "We do those to condition our muscle memory so that, in a match, we can do those spins by habit. Which brings me to one last question: What are you practicing these days, Rick?"

"Okay, man," the younger man admitted, "I'm completely lost where you're going with this."

That was more accurate than Andrew thought was good for the conversation, so he didn't jump on that point. "Right now, you spend most of your days practicing how to wait for something to happen. You're becoming trained at waiting. Your go-to move is now to wait."

"I think you're playing around, man," Rick said slowly, "but I'm not totally sure. I mean, I'm not practicing waiting. I'm just, you know, waiting. I mean, I don't want to rush into anything."

Andrew wasn't going to let him have that one. "Which is, in effect, just waiting. Waiting for friends to decide where to go, waiting for some magic moment to tell you to marry so-and-so, waiting for that big career opportunity. You, my friend, have mastered running out the clock without being called for stalling."

That elicited a sound of some kind from Rick. Whether it was positive or negative wasn't quite clear though.

Andrew kept at it. "What you're no longer a master of – or maybe I should say, what you no longer have an instinct or habit for – is taking charge of the moment."

He waited for a response and, when there was none, he pressed on again. "I want you to prove me wrong here. I just want you to pay attention to the number of times you think or say 'we'll see' or something like that, and how many times you yourself initiate an action, whether it's going out or getting something done."

Still silence on the other end.

"Then we're going to see whether my coaching instincts are right. And if they are, I think I just realized a cool way for you to move forward."

A cool way for Andrew to move forward too.

How excited Rick was, he couldn't tell, though he did end up agreeing to the challenge. But as for Andrew himself? He was ready to take it head on.

CHAPTER 27

Joy Needs a Team

Joanna awoke after a somewhat restful sleep.

At a retreat long ago, she had learned how to serve others when she couldn't sleep at night. She'd simply pray for whoever needed prayers most at that time. In that moment of connecting the person's pain with the relatively mild discomfort of sleeplessness, she was able to create some hope and, in a supernatural way, contribute that hope as well.

The act itself, so simple at first glance, was just a tiny little version of what she was now beginning to understand. Yet it produced a contentment – a joy – that could then help produce sleep.

Produce a contentment.

Wow! That's it.

Joanna thought about those Coeurs workers who had left the company. She reflected how her decisions as a leader had caused them to become discontented, to lose joy.

The rain was now just a slight drizzle. Joanna toyed with whether to spend the next two days there in the woods or whether to just end her camping trip early. The brush with the snake and the nagging thoughts inside her head were a distraction that seemed to be telling her to head back home.

Poking her head out of the tent, she looked skyward. "Okay, are you planning to rain all day?"

She ducked back inside, breathed deeply, and looked at the now damp sleeping bag.

"I think I need to head back," she said out loud. "I don't think I need a third message."

Keeping her tent fly up while she took the larger shelter down and rolled up the ground tarp, she decided to forego making a morning fire. Even though that would mean no hot cup of coffee, Joanna wanted to get into cell range as soon as possible, since she knew she had two brothers who were probably on the verge of calling in the Air National Guard for her.

Carefully watching for snakes the whole time, her morning trek to the car nonetheless gave her time to put the previous day into perspective.

As a pleaser, Joanna had assumed that being a servant-leader was a solitary task. But apparently she wasn't in this alone – not at work or in her personal life. It wasn't up to her to find all the answers herself.

She needed to rely on her fellow team leaders.

That was her insight. Having joy in leadership required her to connect, create, and contribute also. So while, as a leader, her job was to enable joy for those in her charge, she also needed to remember that she had personal connections she could and should rely on to keep her own attitude joyful.

With a sense of mental relief flooding over her as heavily as the rain, she glanced at the sky to see if she was going to get a respite. There was a break in the clouds, and she toyed with the idea of reneging on her decision after all.

Joanna rooted around in her bag and pulled out a Ziploc of granola. Unhooking her water bottle, she asked the Lord to bless her sparse yet nutritious breakfast. Then she set about making a short mental checklist of how to move forward.

Her goal was to somehow transform all her thoughts into practical business applications. And she really did think that with just a little more inspiration – which hopefully didn't manifest itself as another copperhead – she would have it down.

CHAPTER 28

Calendar Clues

Megan made her way to the kitchenette refrigerator to grab her daily bag of fresh cut vegetables, then pulled out her tablet and brought up her Google calendar.

To a very large degree, Megan was pleased that the graphic approach to the joy-in-work drawn up by Dayzie and her seemed to be providing some answers. But as the onslaught of daily emergencies and crises kept predictably piling up on top of her, she wondered how she'd ever be able to keep that focus. It was just too easy to let herself be dominated, and diminished, and maybe even extinguished by the ever-consuming management needs on her plate.

Just checking her calendar was threatening to start that process. She liked everything neat and orderly. That was her happy place, and things were not looking neat and orderly right now.

Her penchant for organization was reflected in the multi-colored array of blocks on her schedule. Each aspect of her day and her project had been duly color-coded so that she could quickly identify priority levels and categories. Red blocks were more critical than the purple ones, and blue ones were her family commitments.

Yet none of it helped her figure out a way to block out time for the very efforts she had awakened her fellow leaders to with her graphic. Her finger scrolled down the calendar. More mosaic-variety, jam-packed days shone on the screen as she did.

What an absolute puzzle!

Megan looked up as she came to the refrigerator, opening the door while still in stride. Grabbing up her zip-top bag of veggies, full of long slices of sweet peppers and carrots, she set her tablet on the table to start snacking, even though her eyes never left that puzzle.

Megan only somewhat heard the voices in the kitchenette: two workers commiserating about how to manage all their children's activities when they got home. The one commented how hard it was to actually have dinner together, which she described as "the most important family time we get all day."

Subtly influenced by the conversation she thought she was doing a decent job of ignoring, Megan looked at the array of blue blocks on her calendar. Sure enough, they were all squeezed down on the bottom of every day, seemingly buried by the purples, reds, oranges, magentas, yellows, and grays.

She pensively munched on another slice, her finger tapping absently on the upper half of the screen.

That's when the idea hit her.

Placing her plastic bag of munchies on the table, she started rapidly reassigning the block colors, being careful that she didn't accidentally delete a commitment in the process. Considering each appointment and task, it took her about fifteen minutes before she stopped and regarded the tablet screen as a whole again.

Then, snatching up her snack, she made a smug little smile at the table and, with long, quick strides, made her way to her next commitment.

Puzzle solved!

CHAPTER 29

A Tool

The email didn't have any content, just a subject line.

Subject: Can you meet on Monday pm; if yes, tell me when you're open.

Her content-less email was yet another way that Joanna tried to save people's time by not even requiring her mail to be opened. But the brevity of the email wasn't an indication that she wanted a brief conversation. She wanted to tell them a lot.

Actually, she wanted to ask them a lot.

Dayzie and Megan were the first to respond, and they both said they couldn't wait. By mid-morning, Andrew, Brian and Nico had also accepted, and the time was set for one-thirty.

Andrew asked if anyone was bringing snacks.

No one responded to that last correspondence, but nobody was much surprised when Andrew arrived to the meeting with a drink, a pear and a banana.

After the general pleasantries were taken care of, Joanna got them officially going with an attention-grabbing announcement. "I am here, but only by about an inch."

The others looked at her with expressions of puzzlement.

"A snake and my boots had an encounter," she explained, "and I was only an inch away from a very different ending to my vacation. The real issue was that I decided to ignore, or not respect, the need to stay connected."

Everyone was still gaping, a fact she enjoyed a little too much. It was the exact reaction she'd been hoping to evoke.

"Thankfully, God taught me a whole new respect for our connect, create, and contribute model." She smiled brightly. "Apparently, I need to rely on you folks to finish the teaching job He started. So this is the part where I'm going to stop talking."

Dayzie had stopped staring sooner than the others.

"Okay. In that case, I think I can start."

"Wow, I'm shocked," Andrew teased.

"She smirked back at him on her way to the whiteboard. "Just to get us on track though," she warned even while she proceeded to lay out a cleaner version of what she was nick-naming "the dual curves."

"This is the point we got our thinking to at last check," she explained. "And I guess that's where I'm going to pass the buck, since I'm still not really sure where to go from there."

Megan chimed in before the resulting silence could get uncomfortable. "I think I have a way to do this with math, using numbers to show what we're doing and why it might be wrong, or suboptimal."

Andrew, using a deep voice and waving his banana like a wand, announced, "And now Megan will turn our employee quitting issue into a math problem. Stay tuned for her next trick, where she'll solve stock market investing with geometry."

Nico half-winced at him in amused skepticism. "You do realize that second part doesn't even make sense, right?"

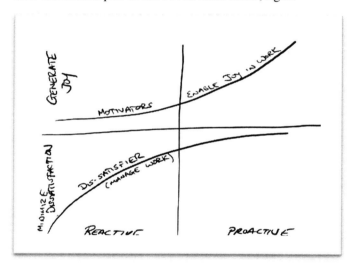

Megan gave a small smile and eyebrow lift, then continued as if there had been no interruption whatsoever. "I need you guys to do a little tally for me," she directed with an instructor's inflections. "But first, I'm going to put a list up on the board."

Joanna took a sip of the coffee she'd made sure to bring with her, watching intently as Megan put it all down.

FIXING TYPICAL PROBLEMS / DEFECTS
PREVENTING TYPICAL PROBLEMS
ANALYZING NON-TYPICAL PROBLEMS
PREVENTING BLACK SWANS / RISK MITIGATION
LOOKING FOR IDEAS
SHARING KNOWLEDGE / NETWORKING
IDENTIFYING RISKS / DOCUMENTING
ANALYZE PROCESS DATA / IMPROVE PROC. (GT)
EXPERIMENTING / PROTOTYPING / BETA-TEST
MENDING RELATIONSHIPS
MENTORING / COACHING
SEARCH for COMMON GROUND / ARGUING

Megan went on. "This is my quick list of what I think we do as leaders and managers. Let's not overanalyze it. Just go with me on it for a bit, because I think you'll see it's good enough as-is, and we can change it later. This is just to illustrate a point."

Andrew looked like he wanted to make a comment but, miraculously, stayed quiet, opting for a bite of his banana instead.

"Take a look at your calendars from last week and try to think where your work hours went," Megan told them.

Joanna didn't bother pointing out that she'd have to think back two weeks. It didn't seem worth interrupting.

"See if you can account for most of your week using these items up here." She pointed to several from the whiteboard list. "For example, I spend at least one hour per day looking at or listening to how projects are going. So I'd start with a five on the analyzing typical problems.

Joanna started writing out each of the items herself.

"Now, I also know I spent pretty close to no time mentoring last week," Megan acknowledged. "I didn't really have any atypical problems, so can't say I spent any time analyzing them. But I did spend a chunk of time writing plans and procedures to prevent problems." She stopped herself, looking around at everyone. "Does that give you the gist of what I'm looking for on this tally?"

Andrew stopped eating with a look of surprise on his face. "Oh!"

Dayzie turned toward him with a slight sense of alarm radiating off her face and form. "What's wrong?"

But Andrew was clearly pleased with whatever thought had just entered his head. "I think we're both bumping into the same concept. But unlike you, I'm off the nerd-hook, since I came to it from a wrestling coach perspective." He waved the last half of the banana. "I think we're going to see that we're good at what we practice day in and day out – and that we may not be all that good at enabling joy in work."

There was a moment of surprised, uncomfortable quiet as everyone traded glances. Then, as if of one accord, they all turned to their mobile devices of choice, looking over their calendars, emails, meeting agendas and meeting minutes: whatever they needed to. Someone would occasionally glance at the ceiling as they made a mental recall of where they spent their time last week, but otherwise, everyone's eyes remained on their data.

When they were all ready, they each took a turn sharing their numbers with Megan, who did a quick tally and then began to put the totals up on the whiteboard.

But Dayzie was to her feet and at the whiteboard before Megan could finish, grabbing up a marker to add the final total.

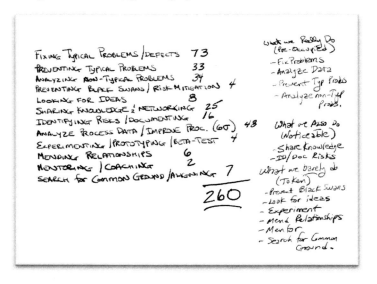

Considering that Dayzie's addition on the board for a few seconds, Megan let out a little "hmm" to herself. "Interesting. Not where I was thinking of going, but it does give me an idea."

She turned back to everyone else. "By putting these into clumps like this, we can see where we're preoccupied: where most of our energy is going. And we can also see, as Dayzie labeled it, what we barely do."

Put like that, it did seem rather damning.

"What I'd like to do," Megan pressed, "is to graphically represent all of this and then somehow map out each task on the dual curves we've got up here already."

Andrew raised his hand.

Megan pointed to him. "Yes, Andrew?"

"I want to continue this. Frankly, this is exactly what I was thinking about on how we can see how well we are enabling joy in work. But, I'd like to run out and bring back some snacks because I think we are going to need some serious brainpower to get this to where we need it to go."

CHAPTER 30

The Tool in Hand

The wasabi peas sounded like rain on a metal roof as they poured into the bowl.

"Here you go," Andrew stated while he moved the healthy yet hot snack to the middle of the table, reserving a fistful for his own consumption. "I brought some to share."

Grabbing a handful, Megan said a quick thanks before going back to Dayzie's original drawing. "Okay, so this area here" – she pointed to the lower-left quadrant – "is the dis-satisfier stuff, or what I sometimes call the management stuff. It's getting rid of problems." She dropped her hand. "We try to get our problems to as near zero as possible, of course, but we always have some, which is why this curve goes asymptotic. We want the least negative."

Joanna jotted that down in case there was going to be a test, which, she supposed, there would be: a real-life one.

"If we took the stuff we do that's about managing and fixing problems, it would be this lower curve," Megan explained, "and we'd realize that while that work is necessary, as the curve shows, it also has diminishing returns. Personally, I think that's what we do as managers; the best you'll get is minimal dissatisfaction, which, as I'm realizing, is not the same thing as satisfaction, and definitely not joy in work."

From Joanna's angle, it seemed like Megan was getting pretty focused on her thoughts, almost to the point where she'd forgotten that the others were even in the room.

"The work we do that helps to connect, or create, or contribute to our vision is on this top curve. This is the work where our motivation – our joy – comes from. And the stuff we do that fits here is what I'd like to think of as our leadership stuff. It's positive and has, as the curve shows, increasing returns."

Blinking twice, Megan appeared to snap out of her trance. "So I'm suggesting we take those tasks, categorize where they fit on these curves, and somehow show the magnitude. We'll then have a visual answer to whether we spend our energy managing problems or enabling joy in work."

Dayzie stood up to grab three markers from the whiteboard: a blue one, an orange one and a yellow one, apparently not caring that they were dry-erase. Then, asking for permission first, she started scribbling task titles on pieces of paper taken from Joanna's notebook.

She wrote the Preoccupied list in black, making the letters as thick and legible as possible. Noticeable went in blue font that wasn't quite as big and bold. And then orange was reserved for the Token list.

Next, she strode over to a filing cabinet on the other side of the room, where she grabbed a roll of masking tape to secure each one to the wall.

While she was ripping and taping, Andrew spoke up. "Well, Megan, I think you did it. You've figured out how to translate motivation, or morale or joy, into a graphical math problem, and I for one, like it. I found that I resonated with the connect, create and contribute, and while I wanted to apply it, I was struggling to figure out how." He gave a small shrug. "While this may not be nailed down with perfect accuracy, it's one heckuva great way to see what we're practicing day in and day out – and, more importantly, what we're not practicing as leaders." Here, he lifted his coffee in a toast. "Seriously, you deserve a big bravo."

Joanna laughed, unable to help herself. "Megan, it looks like you've done more deep-thinking here at the office than I got to do on my little thinking expedition. I'm glad I stopped talking."

Nico got up to help Dayzie, using his fingers as a platform for her to stage the papers with their masking tape strips on. Soon, he had ten notes dangling from his hands.

Dayzie squinted at him. "Okay, here's what I think we could do. I'll put each up where I think it goes, but I won't tape it, and you folks tell me more up, down, right or left. I'll then stick it where we all agree."

The first one took a while, since several of them were mumbling out loud to remember what all was meant by the terms on the drawing. But after what seemed like a long time, the "Fixing Typical Problems" note landed on the lower half of the graph, just about midway but a little to the left.

With some laughter, some frustration and lots of "more up," "more down," "not that much" kinds of comments, each note eventually made its way to an agreed-upon location on the dual curves until Dayzie happily announced, "Last one!" as she put it up.

They all took breaths of relief, then sat or stood there considering the board.

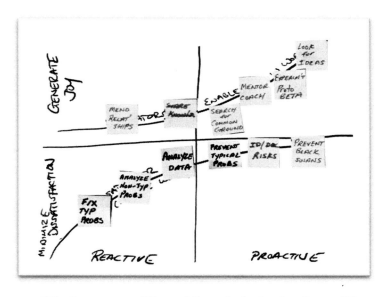

"That's not pretty." It was Nico who broke the silence. "Using Megan's terms, we're doing lots of managing and not much leading. If I thought of it as a car, it's like we've got too much baggage and not enough engine." His face twisted with some mixture of discontentment at the status quo and excitement for the future. "I think we need to start rethinking where we spend our time."

Megan spoke up, a bit softer than usual. "Seeing what we do in this format is a big eye-opener for me. I really believe in the value of that stuff under the line, but now I see it's not getting me what I thought." Her face registered the same complicated expression as Nico. "This is depressing, but in a good way."

Andrew ran a hand over his cropped hair. "I like Nico's metaphor, but what we probably have are too many seatbelts, airbags, big hunks of protective steel, warning lights, cup holders and cushy seats, and not enough of an enjoyment factor. It's like that old Volkswagen ad; it's got no 'fahrvergnügen.'" His hand didn't move from where it had stopped at the nape of his neck. "Lots of time spent just breaking even is what I see on that lower curve."

Megan steepled her fingers together. "I don't know about you guys, but I can see how I've been focusing a lot of energy on making the future supposedly predictable by focusing too much on the dangers underfoot, and not enough on the horizon ahead, which means no new roads to explore with," she looked at Andrew, "that German word you used."

She stayed in her seat but leaned into the table. "But let's not let this data drag us down. All we need to do is figure out how to sell the losers and buy more winners."

Joanna and her fellow team leaders met Megan's words with a bunch of blank stares.

"Are you giving us a recommendation on this enable-joy task or are you giving us some investment advice?" Andrew wanted to know. "You sound more like a stockbroker than a project manager."

"Maybe I'm doing both," Megan laughed. "Think about it. Why do people not sell stock that's plummeting? Because they're connected to the investments. It's a real connection, but ironically, a connection causes them to hold on to those losing stocks and keeps them from thinking about buying stocks that will create better value in their portfolio."

Joanna wasn't following. Connecting was a bad thing now?

"That tendency to connect to what we've already done and already invested in feeds our natural tendency to avoid risk," Megan explained. "As leaders in a time of change, our job is to counteract those natural tendencies. We need to lead by connecting our people to the best ways to create value. We need really focus on that type of leading when that best way may be or look different than the way they are doing it today."

Now that, Joanna could agree with.

"What I'm thinking is that we set the tone: a creative one that paves the way ahead instead of just defending against potential losses. Since folks see where we spend our time, that sends one message. But we may also be able to change our conversation. In other words, there's the time we spend, and then there's the emphasis we communicate. They can be the same, but I don't think they have to be. I guess that's why all the books talk about the need for leaders to have good communication skills."

Nico shifted in his seat. "I think I see where you're going with this. Not to be downer, but keep in mind that we will need to explain this to the Board, if this is what we are agreeing to, in a way that is concise and practical."

Megan nodded. "You're right. I need to think about that. This is about us in our leadership role, not just our management positions. I think that this crazy collage of curves and Post-Its is going to help us be accountable to whether we're actually enabling joy in work." Her eyebrows rose. "I say this while admittedly being a bit nervous. We proved this whole framework hold water; that there's a practical application; that we have a way to hold ourselves accountable. That would seem to give us, especially Tom, an answer to take to the board." Joanna replayed those words in her head for a moment. "Saying that out loud just helped me realize that we do have a powerful answer here. We're not pushing the I believe button anymore. So, I guess my nervousness is just in agreeing with what Nico said; that we serve this up in a concise way for the board."

The rest of the room nodded.

Her hands wrapped around her now-barely warm mug of coffee, Joanna took it all in. It sounded so inspiring in the meeting room, but she knew the process wasn't going to be completely easy or even pleasant. Changing a diaper, after all, came with messy surprises and unpleasant aromas. But that didn't mean it wasn't worthwhile – or that joy couldn't be had in the changing.

CHAPTER 31

Revving

The Mini Cooper kept inching up and down on the hill as Nico gently caressed the engagement point of the freshly repaired clutch until the light changed to green. Then he let it out abruptly, leaving some tread behind on the macadam as he did.

"That's feeling pretty good," Andrew commented. "Why don't you see what happens when you try to start in second."

Nico agreed but decided that a full run through the gear train would be a bit more fun first. He was dying to just let the Mini roar free for a stretch.

Possibly sensing that, Andrew changed the subject. "I think I found a missing link to our enabling joy model of helping our teams to better connect. What I'm realizing is that I have to believe in – that is, connect to – a vision myself before I'm going to be able to help anyone else do it." He drummed his fingers against the passenger door. "I'm not talking about a big corporate vision here. I mean ones that are more closely related to each project. Regardless, I'm starting to think that line about having vision or perish is correct."

"What line is that?" Nico asked as he roughly rode the clutch while shifting into third.

Andrew's head bobbed with the speed shift. "I think it's from Proverbs in the Bible, but I've seen it other places."

Pulling out his phone, Andrew did a quick Google search. "Yup. It's from Proverbs 29 – the first part of verse 18: 'Where there is no vision, the people perish.'"

Nico was both listening to Andrew and for any strange sounds from the car. "So then, you're saying that when you and your team have a vision to believe in, that essentially gives them something to connect to?" He sat up straighter. "Wait. Did you hear that?"

Andrew looked around as if he could see the sound Nico was referring to. "I didn't hear anything except for my fingers drumming on the door."

Feigning annoyance, Nico shook his head. "I've got to find someone else who knows about cars."

"Maybe you do," Andrew grinned. "But back to the whole joy thing, the reason that proverb sticks for me is because it says vision isn't just a nice-to-have; it's a must-have. Without it, you perish. So that made me think hard about whether I've been doing that for my people."

Nico hadn't heard the sound again, so he gave Andrew another piece of his attention, who was still talking regardless.

"I've found that when I focus on making sure we all get the vision – the purpose – it turns my attitude inside out. Face it: we both have little patience for incompetent or lazy people. So I used to just grumble about those people to myself because it eats up too much of my time to try to change them. I used to think that's just how they work, who they are. My evening workouts would be as much about getting in shape as working out my frustrations with those people." He had been sounding dry, but that changed with the next sentence. "But now I'm finding myself trying to flip it around and spend my energy figuring out what I'm doing that's causing them to be disconnected. I'm thinking that laziness comes from not having or even seeing joy in work. In other words, any of us can become lazy if we don't see the joy in work. So I now spend my workouts thinking about what I'm doing or not doing that's causing them to not see joy. I look to see if they're feeling disconnected or unable to create value, or whether I've micromanaged them to the point where they don't see it as their contribution anymore."

"Hmm," Nico said.

"Believe me," Andrew stated, "that isn't easy. But I feel more in control." He stopped himself right there. "No, it makes me more like a coach. And for me, that enables joy in my work."

Nico was now leaning back as the Cooper raced in fifth gear. "I can see that. When I find I personally believe in where we're going, I'm all in." His right hand flexed on the wheel enough to pat it during the silence that followed. "What turned my head on this whole joy in work thing was thinking about why I spent one too many Saturdays working on this car."

"Oh?"

Nico shot him an affirming glance. "Thanks to the crazy engineers at BMW, it's hard, frustrating, and intimidating work. Yet I always look forward to doing it, and I definitely keep on doing it." He smiled at the thought of all that work and how well the Mini was handling now. "I realized it was because I had joy in the process. I wasn't always real happy about it, and I certainly grumbled along the way; but I have to say, I had joy in the work."

Having already heard about his specific adventures those Saturdays ago, Andrew was quick to interject, "It's amazing what wisdom can be gained by fighting a rusted bolt."

Nico snorted. "I was all in: completely connected to the vision that someday, we'd be able to get this thing out on the road – that I'd be creating that reality, and that I'd get to give, or contribute, the effort to my wife."

Finished with that thought, he shot Andrew another glance. "But you're getting the first ride. That way, if my repairs weren't all that great, you can be my roadside service."

Andrew pretended to be offended. "There's always a catch to a free ride."

CHAPTER 32

Proof of Use

Tom evaluated his bike as he fixed the lock on it after his quick lunch ride. It had taken the worst of a little spill the other day while he was pretending to race his son, who was – according to family lingo – zooping on his scooter over some root-heaved sidewalk sections.

He'd thought it okay at the time, but now Tom was thinking it might need a tune up after all.

Later though. For the time being, he had to focus on tuning up some ideas – specifically how to present the joy in work idea at the upcoming board meeting.

Joanna had filled him in on the breakthrough meeting his Buggy Works leadership team had logged, and each one of the team leaders had reached out on their own to tell him how and why they backed her up. In this initiative, they were unified. It was as plain and simple as that.

Personally, Tom was completely aligned with the direction they were headed in. He genuinely believed their seemingly touchy-feely concept had truly pragmatic value. Now it was not only a matter of communicating that to the board, but also proving to them that this approach was what they were looking for. That it could, in fact, be the answer that would re-instill their confidence in the leadership team, and, as a result, the future of Coeurs.

To that end, he wanted to put the story together himself. That way, he'd prove to himself at least that he wasn't just agreeing with the concept, but that he would be ready to responsibly lead its success, and, more importantly, be ready to similarly lead the other Coeurs locations.

With that in mind, he closed his office door and changed his voicemail message to say that he wouldn't be taking calls for the next several hours. Then he mentally situated himself and pulled out his tablet.

Tom called up the appropriate app and began reviewing the notes he'd taken on the board's concerns.

1. Faster pace than our key competitors – improve market share (Need a faster pace or are we faster than competitors and need to maintain that?)
2. Institute a viable and visible continuous improvement strategy, and sustain that strategy (no flavor of the month)
3. Use a structured project management approach to product development and short-term production runs
4. Retain key talent; reduce turnover

At first, Tom groaned a bit as he looked at the list. But the next thing he knew, mild panic was setting in. Because for the life of him, he couldn't see how any of those could be convincingly addressed with the connect, create, contribute approach.

He closed his eyes to tamp down on that rush of alarm, which somehow triggered a very random, but welcome thought. There was a friend of his, Francis, who had spent a lot of his career implementing change and process-improvement efforts. And he might be the perfect resource to utilize.

As luck would have it, Francis not only answered the phone on the second ring, but he said he was free to talk too. So Tom spent some time sharing the details he needed to sort through – the board's challenge, Joanna's idea, his own uncertainty on how to present it – ending with a half-hopeful, half-pessimistic, "So, what do you think?"

The answer wasn't what he was expecting, though maybe he hadn't thought it through that far. The voice on the phone queried:

"Do you have time for a few stories?"

Really, Tom would have rather said no, particularly when he knew how long Francis' stories could be. How he'd forgotten that tendency quirk was beyond him. But it seemed more respectful to say yes, so yes was what he said.

"About ten years ago," Francis began, "I was working with ways to help an onslaught of new hires get a faster jump on learning the art of engineering design and project management. We built it into a game of sorts, where we grouped them into teams.

"At the time, lots of department managers had various back-burner projects that were always in the queue. So we took some of those and doled them out, one to each team. We'd loosely link up the necessary personnel expertise along the way, but it was pretty loosey-goosey otherwise.

"What we found affirmed that enable-joy context you were talking about. The connections and goals they formed were fairly immediate because they were all new hires, so they could relate on that level. Plus, the projects themselves gave them a clear purpose to connect to. And then the fact that they weren't just doing busywork – they could very clearly see it wasn't just an exercise – let them know they were creating value.

"Now, each participant was given a four-hour time budget to work on these projects per week. Yet the hard part was keeping them from pouring in more hours. It was far and away the most engaged new-employee development program I'd ever seen in my more-than twenty years there.

"Moreover, here's what may be the true genius of your enable-joy model: that contribute piece. The little projects we gave them were usually destined to languish – for years, in some cases – because they looked like futile wastes of time or they were just at the very bottom of an ever-building pile. No one thought they would come to pass. But these new hires were told clearly that, if it was a good plan and idea, we'd implement it. They believed all along that there would be a 'contribute' element.

"Get this though. Here's the real proof. Over the years we ran the program, we noticed an ebb and flow of its vitality. And while we had a different way to describe it back then, I now see that its success was linked to all three of the aspects you mentioned. That said, I really think that the 'contribute' part was the real key factor. Because when folks thought their created value would be homeless, it sapped their energy. And now that I'm thinking about it, there were several times we gave them that impression, I'm sorry to say.

"When management added in rules limiting how innovative the teams could be, we diminished their ability to create. And then there were doubters in the leadership sphere who threw additional reviews and roadblocks in the way of making our new-hire creations a reality. It was rather heartbreaking to watch these employees' joy disappear when they ran into barriers set up against their create-value potential."

His story ended just like that, followed immediately by, "You ready for another one?" And Tom found that, surprisingly enough, he really was. He hadn't found himself regretting the phone call once. For that matter, he hadn't found himself doing anything but focusing on the provided example and how he could utilize it.

So Francis continued.

"I also got to be part of a really exciting effort, where we teamed people up from a wide variety of organizations – all of whom were involved in some very complicated industrial platforms. This business had a very clear but complicated need to improve, and this cross-organizational team was an admittedly radical concept for an extreme situation.

"The early days were heady, but the founders hit upon some foundational elements nonetheless. They brought together communities of practice, each one centered a specific key business process. They broke with custom about their meetings, taking them way off-site. Mind you, this took a bit of effort to get the funding for this.

"So right off the bat, each small team was connected by a common business process even though the individual members were from various organizations and levels of hierarchy. We met face to face and dropped all pretense of who was or was not the boss. In other words, we connected. In all sorts of ways. And just like with that new hire program, after some initial floundering, we came up with a very clear purpose, which made us twice-connected.

"Then we were given license to go make it happen, which we did. We created process improvements, better policies – you name it. And because the enterprise was starved for improvements, these ideas and plans got implemented. So we saw that we weren't just some sort of think tank; we were contributors to a better future for the business.

"But guess what? We started to get in our own way, just like the new-hire program. We started trying to formalize this magic recipe we'd created, so we made up all sorts of operating rules and vetting processes to make sure we were working on the right stuff. Worse yet, we created procedures and forced teams to develop annual plans to try to make our magic repeatable.

"Then we committed the ultimate crime: We allowed our organizational leadership to go back to command-and-control mode and teams would go months waiting for this or that approval. You could say we threw blockades all over those connect, create, and contribute parts. Or we disabled joy in our own work."

Realizing the story was over, Tom was just about to say how fascinating those stories were. But Francis wasn't done speaking quite yet.

"This is just my opinion, of course, but both of my stories do seem to jive with what you said. When I hear your enable-joy definition, it makes incredible sense in explaining the ups and downs I saw with those two initiatives."

"Yeah," Tom said. "Thanks for those insights. Those are incredibly affirming."

"Personally," Francis added, "I think your team has found a pretty clever way to explain that 'joy in work' phrase. I'm an old Deming aficionado, so I really appreciate their clear approach. Mind if I steal it?"

That was another welcome affirmation. In fact, the whole conversation had been just what he needed to focus his thoughts. So after they said goodbye, Tom jotted down how his leadership team saw the benefits of the three C's. But that still left him wondering why exactly he believed this would work. The thought was so vivid, that he put it in all caps on his paper.

Because my people do.

It hit him so quickly and clearly that he wondered how he'd ever not seen it. According to their own accounts, each of his Buggy Works team leaders had tested out the theory separately and in their own different ways, yet each of them had come to the same conclusion. Several of them had even moved from doubt to buy-in. But he knew that this was still not sufficient rationale for the board, so he scribbled down the ones that he thought would be.

Tom looked at his notes and liked what he saw. Which meant he was ready to focus exclusively on how to present all of that to the board.

Tom went back to spinning the pen around his finger to let his thoughts come together before grabbing up a blank piece of paper and confidently outlining a board convincing approach.

- Keeps our people engaged → less likely to leave
- Keeps Project Mgmt in Focus → BUT is NOT THE Focus
- Balances Risk & Opportunity management.
- Puts Working on Leading = Working on Managing

→ WHY DO I BELIEVE IT WILL WORK ?!

It makes sense
It's kind of free
Can Start Immediately
Gets to the root of the issue
   Boots on the ground
      It's what we do / not something additional
Helps us see what to change's how
Nice tie with ISO 9001

CHAPTER 33

Facing the Bull

It was board-day, and Tom was mentally prepared for the meeting before him. He had a clear sense of purpose and the conviction to stand behind his words. But he still had to admit that, emotionally, he was pretty apprehensive.

In trying to sort through and get past those concerns, he found himself wondering if the task at hand could be viewed through a joyful lens. Perhaps, he considered, in an almost inverted way since the board was technically there to guide him. Yet most members were focused on the management of Coeurs and, in Tom's opinion, viewed topics like leadership as a necessity, yes, but not a tangible aspect that they needed to bother with.

Or did they just automatically assume it was synonymous with management? That might be the case, particularly with Ellis.

Which meant that Tom had to connect with them in a whole new way – not as the CEO they had selected, but as their leader in teaching them how and why the enable-joy program was worth enacting. He had to treat this meeting not as a way to minimize their dissatisfaction, but as a way to maximize their senses of connectivity, creativity, and contribution.

He was being called to enable joy in the hearts and minds of the very people whose job seemed to be to intimidate him. In that light, Tom supposed he was about to embody the ultimate example of leading without being the boss.

The concept was both humbling and empowering at the same time, and it stuck with him as he grabbed his keys and the handouts he'd compiled, kissed his wife, and told his kids to have a great day, then left to do his very best toward the same.

The first thing he noticed stepping into the board's meeting room was how tense it was in there. There was the usual professional courtesy and respect displayed as greetings were exchanged, but it was still tense nonetheless. That tone didn't come as any shock, particularly when Ellis directed a demanding stare at him as soon as he walked in.

No doubt, he had already made at least a few comments to everyone else about his expectations and the consequences that would come if the resident CEO failed to meet them.

Tom took his place at the end of the table, where he immediately passed the stack of stapled handouts to the somewhat diminutive, quiet gentleman on his right, Dr. Alex Van Buskirk.

As an acclaimed medical implant surgeon, the doctor was the prominent profession-specific voice on the board, providing key insights on how to approach the design and testing processes for Coeurs' main line of medical devices. The man was usually very quiet in the meetings themselves though, since he and everyone else there knew he wasn't a businessperson. Instead, Dr. Van Buskirk tended to voice his ideas during sidebar conversations or during breaks.

He had a way of working his ideas gently and respectfully into conversations that often swayed listener's opinions in the end. For now, he just gave Tom a welcoming nod while he accepted the stack of papers.

Tom took a sip of water from the glass he'd already gotten himself. And then he got down to business while the handouts continued to make their rounds.

"Thank you all for being here. It's my pleasure to share what I have with you today. I'm sure you were expecting to see an array of well-designed, thought-provoking ideas all sanitized into a neat parade of bullet points."

Everyone looked at him expectantly.

"But I'm not going down that route," Tom told them. "What you have in front of you doesn't look that organized, I know. But it's everything you'll need to document my recommendations of how Coeurs can – and will – exceed your expectations in explicitly and continuously improving, and managing our product development and delivery processes."

No matter that there were already several skeptical looks around the table. Tom felt himself strengthening in his role of presenter and leader.

"We've discovered that we're not living up to the core concepts Coeurs was founded on thirty years ago. Despite living out the laws of servant leadership as we saw fit, we weren't, in the words, more of less, of Dr. W. Edwards Deming, 'enabling joy in work.'

"In order to realize this, we had to first approach the facts with an open mind. And we didn't see the need to do that until we noticed key talent walking out the door and started listening to water cooler conversations, which didn't sound particularly satisfied.

"Personally, I wanted to just mandate some sort of resolution for these problems. I wanted to manage them away with a dose of good old-fashioned command and control; and so did a few of my best team leaders. But the leadership team at our Pennsylvania facility decided to approach the issue very differently. They took a hard look at what they had and had not been doing as leaders since Coeurs began implementing this board's recent resolutions."

There were varying levels of expectation being displayed across various faces in front of Tom while he reached for his water again, then set it back down.

"When the program manager there presented her thoughts to me," he picked up again, "I appreciated it – but in the same way I appreciate a good sermon. It all sounded like motherhood and apple pie to me. So I challenged her to translate it into a practical process instead of a list of high-sounding concepts to be plastered on a poster in the passageways.

"It was a challenge she and the team leaders under her took up with a will and a way. And in so doing, they realized that they were indeed connected with this board's intended purpose for them to improve and manage better; but that the way they were going about it was resulting in some undesired outcomes – outcomes that were the very opposite of what we all really wanted.

"Therefore, what they proposed and what I am proposing today, should make perfect sense to you in concept. In many ways, it will clarify what you've believed but maybe couldn't put into a practicable process. And that's what my deciding factor was in bringing their collective idea forward as my own recommendation to address your challenges: the idea of always measuring how well we're enabling joy in work."

Two people down and on his left, Ellis' expression changed from skeptical to downright irritated.

Tom turned away and pushed on.

"Too often, even Deming's most faithful students can take the term 'enable joy in work' superficially," he explained. "We all just nod our heads and agree with how nice it sounds, even if we have no idea how to translate it into a day-to-day tool. Yet what we're putting into practice at our Pennsylvania facility is a way to move from Sunday sermon to Monday meaningfulness.

"That's what the program manager set out to do in the first place, and her resulting insights inspired five of the team leaders to test the ideas and advance them into a tool. The tool is a way for each of us to stand back and assess how well we're leading." He paused to let that sink in, then added, "Notice how I said 'leading,' not 'managing.' We have all the numbers and graphs we need to assess work management. What we were lacking was a way to assess how well we lead people. And we now have a way to do that.

"If you flip to page five of your handout, you'll see this illustrated. But let me explain it to you personally as well. I need you to believe it, not just know it. This tool provides a way for us to take a look at our priorities, where we spend our valuable time, and how much of that time we spend on managing versus leading – to see where we spend our time on resolving problems and achieving measurable perfection versus how often we're pursuing greatness, with 'greatness' being defined as 'joy in work.'"

Ellis let out a distinctive snort, which Tom didn't let slow down his momentum.

"We've explicitly defined that joy in work is a function of being connected to the purpose and people of Coeurs, being able to create value to that purpose, and seeing that value contribute to and benefit our customers. As you can see on page six, we can actually quantify how much effort we spend on those elements. And thanks to this analysis, when we see a lack of joy in work, we can acknowledge that we're failing at our job as leaders – even if we're excelling at our work as managers. This was one of the many realizations we came to while we wrestled with answering the challenges you put forth.

"Just by doing this assessment, we're now able to step back and reevaluate how we're engaging, encouraging, and implementing our project management processes and performance improvement initiatives. That transforms them from being compliant directives to being truly helpful practices. And that's a key difference: one that helps to retain, and even excite, our people, especially those we most rely on." Tom found himself leaning forward into his presentation. That's how much he believed in it. "It also has a much more tangible outcome when it comes to how we meet and exceed our customer expectations."

Despite his own connection to the presentation, he could tell not everyone was feeling the same. And it wasn't just Ellis who still needed to be swayed. While that unhappy individual looked like he'd already made up his mind about everything, there were several other members registering flashes of disgruntled discontent across their faces and forms.

That gave Tom two options: either to backtrack in an effort to explain everything from a different angle, hoping to help them connect that way, or to soldier on in hopes of swaying them still.

He went with the latter.

"So how do we actually implement this? You'll see that question explained on pages eight to ten of your handout. Once again taking a note from Deming, we found a way to translate his Plan, Do, Study, Act learning cycle into a way to help us lead change by enabling joy and assisting our teams to connect, create, and contribute.

"So that is my recommendation, ladies and gentlemen. It's actually our Pennsylvania facility's recommendation as well, since the good leaders there are already well onto implementing this path. Together, we firmly believe we've found the key to answering your directives. And it all came down to a better leading strategy and the act of enabling joy in work."

With that, he stopped talking and braced himself to listen.

CHAPTER 34

Taming the Bull

"You really expect us to believe that's going to work?"

Not surprisingly, it was Ellis who spoke first, and he was visibly agitated.

"You're the most inept person we've ever hired!" He held out his hands in exasperation. "Why don't you just admit you're in over your head and save yourself the embarrassment of us canning you!"

Tom heard him, but he wasn't just focusing on Ellis' obvious reaction. He was also studying the other faces around the table. A few of them did appear to agree with their raging colleague, but most of them looked disgusted or embarrassed by his behavior.

Unaware of that or, more likely, unconcerned about it, Ellis was in the process of opening his mouth to speak again.

"You appear upset," a calm voice to Tom's right noted, making him swivel in surprise. His first mental reaction was

196 PAUL F. ARMSTRONG

that it couldn't be who he thought it was. Yet there Dr. Alex Van Buskirk was nonetheless, looking straight at Ellis like he was waiting for a reply.

Everyone else appeared startled too, including Tom's key antagonist.

"I'm not upset," Ellis managed anyway. "I'm doing my job and calling this ridiculous idea and its incompetent owner out for what they really are." The more words he let out, the more he seemed to recover his bluster. "I'm clearly the only one here who has the guts to think this through, come out and flag this stupid plan."

If Dr. Van Buskirk was fazed, he didn't show it. "The reason I asked if you were upset is because I'm sincerely worried your body chemistry is working against the intelligent type of thinking you're challenging us to have."

If anyone else had said it, it would have come across as inexcusably insulting. Yet he somehow managed to express it mildly, as if it was just one more concept to consider. So, astounding though it was, Ellis let it slide and allowed Dr. Van Buskirk to continue.

"That aside, with your permission, I'd like to share how I'm understanding what Mr. Waldmor is proposing."

The rest of the board seemed ready to listen. And Ellis even went so far as to nod, proving that miracles could, in fact, happen.

Dr. Van Buskirk's small, fit frame somehow took on a more commanding presence. "Even though I may not know about project management or process improvement, I do know about what makes people healthy – what makes them function better.

And what I've heard from Mr. Waldmor is exactly that: a way for both those who lead and those who follow to be healthier."

While listening to him, Tom noticed one previously skeptical expression soften further down the table.

"It matches what we've been learning and relearning in the health business for years: that what matters most is for people to be connected to others and to a purpose. Mr. Waldmor's approach simply lays that out as a foundation for how Coeurs' employees can practice that necessity day to day." His head moved slowly as he spoke, including everyone into his analysis. "I appreciate that focus. While I admit to not fully understanding all the details behind his plans to enable joy, as a doctor, I do understand that when people can create and contribute to a purpose, their mental health is better. And that translates very directly to better physical health.

"Those results alone seem to be a good enough business case for us to consider Mr. Waldmor's idea as a valid platform. To wax a bit philosophical, his idea emphasizes the 'human' in HR instead of the 'resources.'"

He wasn't looking at Ellis when he continued, his presentation as non-confrontational as it was direct. "I don't see this plan as stupid, but as elegantly simple. It's not a big rollout with expensive training – and we've all heard the complaints about those approaches. Yet it appears to patch the gaps in how process improvement and project management are rolled out without taking anything away from those efforts."

Tom allowed himself the smallest of smiles. It appeared he'd at least connected with one person, and that one person was doing a great job connecting with others. Hadn't Joanna said something about not having to lead alone?

"Actually," Dr. Van Buskirk persisted, "it sounds like it can only help those efforts. We, the board, asked for answers to a tough problem. We did not get excuses, rationalizations, some big management plan, or a parade of consultants. We got something that builds on who Coeurs is and what Coeurs has, not to mention something that would seem to make financial sense."

By all appearances, Ellis appeared to be considering what was being said.

"So far, I see no reason not to endorse this plan."

And with that, he gave up the floor.

There was an air of impressed silence for several seconds before one of the more aggressive members weighed in. "Tom, how would you propose we monitor the success of this program? It does sound like it has merit, but are there ways to measure its progress step by step?"

Tom nodded, having already contemplated such a question. "There are a number of factors you could review month by month, each one a sign of corporate health: employee turnover, new product introductions, the speed from concept to market. Each one could and should show whether we're enabling joy in work, and opening the means to connect, create, and contribute across the Coeurs enterprise."

Someone else moved his hand from his chin. "How many months would you be asking for to prove the success of this theory?"

Tom answered that one as well, and the next one, and the next, each sounding less and less skeptical until a clear common ground could be found. For once, the divisive and antagonistic Ellis didn't rule the day. He even engaged in the conversation, suggesting pragmatic approaches for how the enable-joy proposal could be communicated to potentially skeptical investors.

Leaving the boardroom that afternoon, Tom mentally went through his list of goals for the meeting.

Connect? Check.

Create? Check again.

Contribute? I think so.

It looked like he was on his way to enabling joy at Coeurs.

CHAPTER 35

Taking It Home

The chocolate was still soft as Megan used her fork to cut off another piece of made-from-scratch buttermilk pancakes. They were her husband's handiwork and standard Saturday morning fare for the family.

While the girls always got smiley-face pancakes, the ones meant for Megan were oblong to maximize skillet usage. Sometimes, she found, her spouse was as fastidious about being efficient as she was.

Said husband was currently washing the dishes, and their daughters had long-since gulped down their breakfast. So they were now busy with their morning chores. Megan, however, had chosen to savor every single bite, so she was alone at the table, scrolling through her calendar app.

She was still sticking with her new color-coding scheme that basically let her see how each day could either lead to enabling joy or just dealing with crises and administrative tasks. What she'd found was that various chunks of time she'd originally thought were joy killers could be transformed into joy enablers. Many times, it was just a function of the language she used; in other cases, it was in how she set expectations.

Yet one way or the other, the enable-joy model was more down-to-earth and doable and applicable than she'd initially imagined. Because of it, she was realizing that telling her kids to "clean your teeth" as opposed to "brush your teeth" made the task sound more purposeful and valuable. And "let's dress" implied more connecting and creating than "get dressed."

Sure, it did require her to change some habitual perspectives and language choices, but it was resulting in entirely better outcomes.

That had shown so well on Friday evening, when she went out to run errands with her daughters. Normally, Megan had the same efficiency with her shopping routines as she did with her work projects. That's why she rarely bought from brick-and-mortar retailers, finding the online options to be a better use of her time. But what she was discovering was that seemingly mundane tasks could be turned into joyful tasks by incorporating time with her daughters. Shopping took a little bit longer, true, but so much more was gained.

Unfortunately, that habit had her completely discounting how the Christmas shopping season was in full swing. And she had regretted not accounting for the additional crowds, joking with herself that she'd failed to do adequate risk management and have a mitigation plan before implementation.

However, she hadn't let that mistake trump her parental instincts to nurture her children, even if that meant a few unplanned trips down other aisles in the stores.

Enabling joy in work didn't come at the cost of being efficient. It just relegated efficiency to a different priority, acknowledging that effectiveness was considerably more valuable and desirable.

Closing the tablet, she smiled and went to go help out her husband. They had a lot of outdoor activities planned for the day, and the sooner they cleaned up, the sooner they would be hearing the giggles of two girls.

CHAPTER 36

Taking It to Heart

Joanna kept her promise to herself and left the office with enough time to stop for a short stroll in the county park. Despite it being December in Central Pennsylvania, the temperature was in the fifties, which made for extremely comfortable hiking weather. The days might be shorter, but the weather was lovely.

The place was full of trails that wound their way through wooded areas, enticing walkers to believe they were far away from civilization even though the park was actually very much in the city.

Pulling into the gravel lot, Joanna wasted no time readying for the walk since it was already dusk. She swung her feet out of the car and, reaching behind her, grabbed her hiking boots to put them on.

They made her smile, even if she didn't slow down in tying them up. There were only very small marks left from where the snake had bitten, with the soles seemingly healed over the holes.

"Sort of metaphoric," she said out loud.

A lot had changed at work since Labor Day. While it was still much too early to call what was now officially known as the Enable Joy Method an out-and-out success, the Happy Factor Index had nonetheless stopped its downward trend. Of course, that could just be a Christmas season excitement bump. But she, the leadership team, Tom, and the board were all steadily gaining confidence that enabling joy was more than just a slogan.

She was also realizing it was a journey that spoke to her personally – first and foremost about having faith in her peers, and then also about humbly serving them with her ideas. The fruit of that faith and humble service was, profoundly, joy.

Joanna only walked for a short time, and even then, she needed her phone to light the last fifty yards back to the car. But it was enough to enjoy; and besides, her mind was already well into preparing for what would be her last religious education class before the Christmas break.

Turning off the flashlight app, she happened to catch her administrative panel, which showed five bars. Total reception.

It made her grin as she slid into the car, the memories of her Labor Day hike coming back to her as *Joy to the World* played in her head once again. The tune that had started it all – and now it was almost time to really sing it, as Advent was coming to a close.

In just a few hours, she would be sharing the different birth accounts as found in the gospels of Luke and Matthew, and then tying it up with the beautiful incarnation poem that served as the first chapter of John.

> **John 1:1-5**
> *In the beginning was the Word, and the Word was with God and the Word was God. He was in the beginning with God. All things came to be through him, and without him nothing came to be. What came to be through him was life, and this life was the light of the human race; the light shines in the darkness and the darkness shall not overcome it.*

At her first class this year, she had enjoyed shedding some new light on the Creation story they had heard since first grade. She explained how God invited the human race to have dominion. That intrigued the students how this was at the start of the Bible, which they were constantly reminded was the most powerful love story.

This time around, as soon as class began, Joanna was very quick to tell them to get out their pens for an exam, watching how nervous everyone immediately got. She dragged it out a few additional seconds for the suspense factor.

"Okay, here's the exam. Ask me one good question."

Most of them stared at her, obviously waiting for more, while her most dutiful students were still writing down what she'd said, thereby really missing the point.

It was one particularly intelligent but skeptical young lady, Sarah, who finally responded. "Why are you here?"

By the exact tilt of her smirk, it was clear she thought she was being pretty clever asking the same kind of wide-open question that Joanna frequently asked the class.

Joanna smiled back. "Why am I here? Why do I do this? Why do I give up my evenings to come here when I could do other things at home or with my friends?" She looked around the room. "Well, I find that there's a certain beauty – let's call it joy – in helping all of us see this thing we call faith a little more clearly and connecting with it in a deeper way."

Sarah was already looking a little disappointed that she hadn't stumped the teacher.

But Joanna wasn't finished. "Did you know that the word 'religion' means to hold together? It comes from the same word as ligament, that stuff that holds our bones together. So religion is sort of the spiritual ligament that holds us together as people."

She let herself study the children's faces as they processed that information. "Our faith. That's what holds us together to be better at living the life that our loving Creator has given us – a joyous life. Joyous, not in that we'll fill every minute with laughter, but joyous in a contented kind of connectedness with Him and with each other."

That deserved a pause, but even so, Joanna still wasn't quite finished. "And hopefully, being better connected isn't just the reason I'm here, but the reason all of you are here too. Even though I may be called the teacher, I walk out of here with a new perspective on our faith every week." She looked directly at their faces. "I hope that's true across the board."

Sarah shrugged as if it didn't matter much, but there was more than one indication that she was happy with the expanded answer.

When they ran out of questions, Joanna compared Jesus' birth accounts in the Gospels of Matthew and Luke, and them compared it to the beginning of the Gospel of John. When she was done, she looked up from the Bible. "Here's your Christmas break homework," Joanna instructed. "Go enable joy in your home. Try to connect with your friends and relatives – maybe your brother or sister – in a new way. If they're far away, then call them or, at least Facebook them," she added to cover any excuses the kids could come up with. "Then, see if you can create a Christmas memory, a Christmas moment. That will be your holiday contribution: an act that touches a heart."

Her eyes twinkled at her very last directive. "So there we go. Go forth and bring joy to your world!"

Saying goodbye to each of them in turn, Joanna took in their expressions, and chatter, and laughter as they left the classroom. It was just as rewarding as their participation during each class. They were a joy, and so was sharing her time with them.

Really, she noted as she got into her car, they were an affirmation of her earlier thoughts. Having faith in them and in the message she shared, serving them, and serving the Word all produced the fruit of joy.

As if on cue, *Joy to the World* started up in her head again, making her shake her head in amusement. Yet a funny thing happened on the second time around. She found herself singing the words out loud and in a new sequence.

"The Lord has come. Joy to the world."

And her brain didn't stop there, tumbling words and their meanings around as if it had been created for that sole purpose.

The Lord.

Dominus.

My head of the household.

My boss has come. Joy to my world!

That had her laughing all over again as she pulled into her driveway. It looked like that song was never going to mean the same thing to her. And thank God for that!

Her first self-appointed task once inside was to pull out some violet-themed stationery to write a long-overdue thank you note to the monastery – her own version of the very homework she'd given to her students.

After that was signed, sealed, and ready for the mail, she heated up a cup of non-caffeinated Ethiopian and made sure to add in a generous sploosh of eggnog. Then, sitting in her favorite chair, hugging her cup, and sipping slowly, she savored a contented peace and the knowledge that there really was joy in the world – and the work – that could be found.

There was a book on the table beside her, and it called out to be finished. A tempting notion, Joanna savored the idea of disappearing into its thought-provoking prose. Yet as her hand reached for it, her fingers instead found her phone. It showed a very strong four bar signal.

She smiled. The book would wait. And within seconds, she was fully connected with her brothers in a cheerful, heartfelt conversation.

Joy to the World
The Lord is Come
Let earth receive her King

Joy! Yes sisters Joy is in humble service and I am learning that. Thanks to my time there, I have learned anew that when I lead as a believer, I need to be Christ to others, to reflect the image and likeness that we are made in. Just as the angels announced Joy to the World with the coming of the King, so too my duty as a leader is to enable joy in our world of work. Enable Joy. Our King whom we await this advent brings joy to the world. Our Lord, Dominus, enables joy. So too must I.

Gloria in Excelsis Deo.

VJ
Joanna

Meet the Cast

With a guess at their Myers Briggs preferences.

Joanna – an intuitive data gatherer who makes relational decisions, prefers internal energy. A fairly clear INFP.

Dayzie – in intuitive data gatherer who makes logical decisions, can take a mess and organize it, prefers external energy. Very likely an ENTJ.

Andrew – intuitive data gatherer with a strong ability for sensory data, a logical decision maker but not at the expense of maintaining relationships. Probably an ENTP.

Nico – a sensory data gatherer who favors practical, logical decision making. A fairly clear ISTP.

Megan – a sensory data gatherer with a preference for logical, linear decision making, the uber utilitarian, also has a knack for relational decision making. Probably an ISTJ or ISFJ, but she might be an INTJ.

Tom – an intuitive data gatherer but revels in lots of sensory data (research); prefers logical decision making yet keeps the relational decision making at the fore. Lots of reasons to think he's an INTP.

Mr. Ellis – a nervous, self-important, brow beating hot head – don't be this guy.

Dr. Van Buskirk – hard to tell, but a relational decision maker, probably intuitive data gatherer, could be that rare INFP.

Brian, Brandon, Pat, Rod and Sarah…too minor to tell.

Francis – an ENFP, I know that for sure.

QuickGuide to Enabling Joy

Overview

This is quick guide on **how to lead by enabling joy.**

Keep in mind. This is just a quick overview. Ideally, you got all the cool nuances of enabling joy from the adventures of Joanna, Tom, Andrew, Dayzie, Megan, Nico and even Mr. Ellis and Dr. Van Buskirk.

My discovery of enabling joy as our calling as leaders is based on a twenty year journey working with teams and team leaders at work, home, church and play. The journey is personal and professional, spiritual and intellectual. While the fable does justice to how the journey really occurred, this QuickGuide version will put in practical terms a discovery that was clearly a gift of the Holy Spirit, not a well planned pursuit that I can take credit for.

This is NOT a book on leadership traits.

The focus is what to DO as a leader, not who to BE.

There are clearly traits that are critical for leading well, for being a servant leader. Actually, they are the same traits we'd like to see in most everyone, so of course they are even more valuable when called to lead. I subscribe to the principles of Servant Leadership, as well described by Robert Greenleaf. If that's not your style, then maybe you should stop here and read Machiavelli.

But again, expounding on leadership is not what this book is about.

This book is about leading by enabling joy, so maybe I should start by explaining why leaders are called to enable joy in work.

Mother Theresa stated, "Joy is Strength." As leaders, isn't our deep desire to strengthen those on our team? Isn't that what our leadership should be providing?

Enabling joy provides strength by opening the capacity to connect, create and contribute.

Another benefit when we enable joy is a type of peace that could be called deep contentment. The term contentment shares the same confusion as the term joy. Just as joy can be easily mistaken as merely being happy, contentment can be superficially understood as being satisfied, like how we feel after a delicious meal. Deep contentment is when we not only have that feeling that we have sated our hunger, but when we feel the nourished strength to go out and do it again.

Seeing how enabling joy provides a deep contentment type of peace provides us a way to see the opposite of enabling joy, i.e. discontentment. That discontentment can be portrayed by the image of the frustrated athlete sitting on the bench. While the coach can preach the critical role of those who ride the pine, down deep there is a frustration, a discontentment. Why? Because, while on the bench, the athlete does not see herself or himself connecting, creating and contributing to the same degree as his teammates in the game.

Many of you have experienced the transformational excitement that comes with enjoying work. Recall what it was like. If your experiences are like mine, when we enjoy our work, we want nothing more than to do our best, to be a helpful team member, and to see the smiles on all the faces, workers and customers, when we deliver the fruits of our labors.

Five Building Block Assumptions

To set the playing field, here are assumptions *Enabling Joy* automatically makes about leading, managing, the reasons why we lead, and how this guidebook is just one part of a bigger picture.

As you'll see, each one builds off of the next.

Assumption #1 - First and foremost, leading is about enabling joy

Managing, meanwhile, is about delivering predictable excellence. Truth be told, you're probably called to do BOTH of these jobs. The trick is when to do one versus the other.

Given that you're reading this book, you probably have two jobs; one is to lead, the other is to manage. The way I simplify the distinction is this: Leading is about enabling joy in work; it's about the people around the table. Managing is about making excellence predictable and repeatable; it's about the work on the table.

Assumption #2 - Leading is about change

Leading initiates and guides people to and through change, while managing provides predictability and stability.

Assumption #3 - Leaders serve to make life better

The changes that leaders lead are initiated for the purposes of improvement, be those personal or organizational, or both.

Assumption #4 - Enabling joy leads to delighting customers

In service situations, enabling joy in work directly drives customer delight. For production situations, the linkage is looser, but linked nonetheless. Enabling joy in work achieves good outcomes for all of our constituents, payers and payees.

Assumption #5 – Enabling joy is important; satisfying needs is necessary

In the world where work is compensated, we often misuse that compensation, be it pay, title, benefits, or security, as drivers or motivators. These elements for safety, security and sustenance are like breathing, necessary for living but not the purpose of living. You will see this explained later.

Enabling Joy: Explained

Enabling joy.

Naturally, I love that phrase. After all, it's the name of this book! I was turned on to this concept from two very different sources.

The first source is the Bible. To give you a glimpse. From the Gospel of Luke 2: 8-11 (NABRE). (bold is my emphasis)

> *Now there were shepherds in that region living in the fields and keeping the night watch over their flock. The angel of the Lord appeared to them and the glory of the Lord shone around them, and they*

were struck with great fear. The angel said to them,
"Do not be afraid; *for behold, I proclaim to you*
*good news of **great joy** that will be for all the people.*
For today in the city of David a savior has been born
*for you who is **Messiah and Lord**.*

Intrigued? I hope so.

The second source is a series of statements made by the father of the modern quality movement, W. Edwards Deming. He made most of these towards the end of his very long and influential career. He talked about the aim of management. What did he say?

"The aim of management…is to enable everybody to enjoy his work."

"…should be to create a system in which everybody may take joy in his work."

"…to create an environment where everybody may take joy in his work."

In conversations along the way, I (and others) combined these quotes into this concise phrase: A leader's job is to enable joy in work.

Wow. The Lord is come. Joy to the world. As leaders, our calling is enabling joy. Let's unpack why this is so exciting.

Start with Genesis

From the NABRE version, Genesis 1:26-28,31. (bold is my emphasis)

> *Then God said: Let **us** make human beings in our image, after our likeness. Let them have **dominion** over the fish of the sea, the birds of the air, the tame animals, all the wild animals, and all the creatures that crawl on the earth.*
>
> *God **created** mankind in his image; in the image of God he created them; male and female he created them. God blessed them and God said to them: Be fertile and multiply; fill the earth and subdue it. **Have dominion** over the fish of the sea, the birds of the air, and all the living things that crawl on the earth... God looked at everything he had made, and found it very good. Evening came, and morning followed— the sixth day.*

Now, we could fill a whole book interpreting this passage, but I'm going to focus on four words that I believe are key: dominion, us, create and good.

Dominion isn't a word we see much today, but don't be fooled. It has great depth of meaning. It's based on the Latin "dominus," which means "head of the household." It can also be translated as "serving leadership of." So, to have dominion is not to dominate or to lord it over others. To have dominion is to be a servant leader.

"Us" is a very simple, not particularly compelling word, yet it represents something very important to humans: connectedness and community. None of the other creative days have this reference to "us." When creating humankind, the verse is "Let **us** make..." This is the first clue of the Trinity, since it reveals that God is connected – connected as Father, Son and Holy Spirit. From this we can see that the basis of dominion, or being a servant leader, comes from being **connected**.

"Create" is arguably the word that best sums up the Genesis narrative. All throughout, God creates, showing us that this strangely complex world of ours comes with a necessary **creative** dimension.

"Good" is the end goal. Just like God on each of the creative days, we want to look at what we've done, what we've created, and find it good. We want to know that we've brought good into the world and to basically give that good to others. God exemplifies this when He says "Let them have dominion..."

Basically, we, as people, have built into our very being the calling to **contribute** what we create.

All fascinating, you might be saying... But why is this in a book about leading?

Because right here in Genesis, God set out a guide for all leaders. Even as He gives man dominion, He gives man everything he needs to know in order to exercise that dominion properly. And the end result? Look back at what that angel said in the account by Luke. The angel announced that the Lord – the boss, the leader – is coming. That's news that brings great joy.

If you're still with me, then you see that the calling of a leader is to enable joy to their world, the place where he or she has the gift of dominion. Which now begs a few new questions:

How do we start enabling joy, especially joy in work?

What does joy in work look like?

The Three C's

To pull the Genesis interpretation into everyday terms, I needed a picture. Here's my picture of joy in work as originally seen in the previous story you may or may not have read. (Yes, I drew it myself):

Just in case my drawing skills leave you confused about what's going on here, this is a depiction of a woman changing a baby's diaper.

Why?

Because this is a job. It's work. It's literally stinky, messy work. As such, it isn't a task we wake up in the morning hoping to do more of. But it's a fundamentally necessary task that's part of a calling. A vocation. And once the work is done, there is joy in having done it. So how does this unpleasant, mundane task bring joy to the doer?

Let's consider what the work really involves, no matter how removed it may seem from your leadership role right now.

- We have an intimate **connection** between two people.
- We have a clear understanding of why we are doing this work, that is, we can **connect** to its purpose. |
- We have a person clearly **creating** value, converting unhappy to happy.
- We have the creator of that value (who could just as easily be a man as a woman) **contributing** that value, in essence, giving it away.

There is JOY in this work because we have work that **connects, creates and contributes**.

Let's unpack each of those three terms.

Connect
Why does a leader need to enable connecting?

This is the *sine qua non* – or essential component – of enabling joy in work. The ability and willingness to connect is the underlying intrinsic motivation that leaders must promote.

As people, we need and long for connection to others. Studies continually affirm that connectedness is the key factor in a long happy life, in mental health, and in organizational productivity. From Grant Study, a 75-year-long Harvard study on adult happiness as talked about by Robert Waldinger, Director of the Laboratory of Adult Development at Massachusetts General Hospital, to the Google teaming study in 2012 called Project Aristotle.

We need to be connected. To others. To purpose.

This means that your job as a leader is to enable your people to be and stay connected to their colleagues and to their goals.

More than likely, you're familiar with the statistic that shows how people typically leave their jobs due to some disconnect with their bosses or peers, not because of pay, office size, or benefits. While it's true that those extrinsic components may play a supporting role in their workplace unhappiness, the initial driver to look elsewhere most of the time is broken connectedness.

We don't just need to be connected to our team but also to the team's purpose. We long to connect to a purpose bigger than ourselves or outside of ourselves.

We all strive to have meaning in our lives – a purpose for our passion and our perspiration. Thousands of books on managing and leading resonate on the value of creating a shared vision and common mission, complete with some compelling statement that aligns the purpose of why the organization exists and what its dreams are. While there's a lot of cynicism around vision and mission statements, much of which is well earned, there is a fundamental rightness to the concept. It's a matter of the leader being able to visibly promote the purpose and effectively communicate why it's worth being connected to, and not a matter of catchy phrase.

Remember Assumption #2? It's the one that claims that leaders have a fundamental, critical role in taking people through change.

What happens during times of change that makes leading, rather than just managing, so critical? Relationships, purposes and/or routines are modified and redirected, each and any of which are excellent breeding grounds for team members to get or feel **disconnected**. What he or she could rely on yesterday might not be so reliable tomorrow. Change necessitates a disconnection from the status quo and that's why it's so important for leaders to promote connectedness to the new way.

As leaders then, it's your first priority to offer a steady stream of encouragement to refocus: a new shared vision that offers the same kind of connection in the end. When employees have to let go of their comfortable habits, they need, more than ever, to feel connected to what their new purpose is and to know that they're not alone.

Create
Why does a leader need to enable creating?

This is where the dream, the purpose we are connected to, transforms from idea to reality. It's where we transform raw inputs into valuable outputs.

The term "create" sometimes evokes the mental image of being creative, and many of us dismiss ourselves as not being creative, limiting the definition to artistic or musically inclined. But our term "create" can and should encompass so much more than that. Consider the diaper example given before. We create a solution to a problem, we create comfort where there was distress, we create happiness where there was crying, we create freshness where there was stinkiness.

Deming had a way to portray this term create and it was with a simple graphic that has become known as the SIPOC. In essence, all work should be defined as the process when supplied inputs get converted, via what he calls a process, to create outputs that are valued by customers.

The SIPOC connection – For those of you experienced in quality or process improvement, you know of the common picture (which Deming first used in the 1950's) that shows work as a process: Suppliers, Inputs, Process, Outputs, Customers Abbreviated as SIPOC. This creation element is the center-piece of SIPOC, the P, where we create value by transforming inputs into outputs that serve customer needs.

Thinking back to the Genesis account, we see the ultimate creative action, from nothingness to all universal existence. And we see that, being made in the image of the Creator, we have a calling to create.

As a leader, your job is to enable, or, as I like to think of it, unleash that calling to create, that creative passion, that creative role. Some of that role is managerial in nature, assigning talents to task in a sensible way. Most of that task is about helping each person see himself or herself as creating value, as being vital parts of the endeavor at hand. Like an orchestra conductor, we must enable each musician to collectively create the symphony, no matter how many notes each one will play.

Contribute
Why does a leader need to enable contributing?

Contribute. This verb is derived from Latin root words meaning to bestow together or to bring together. Looked at that way, it's not hard to see how it circles right back to the necessity of connecting.

To quote Deming, *"Joy on the job comes not so much from the result, [or] the product, but from the contribution."*

This is where the task becomes a treasure.

Keep in mind that contributing is not the same as delivering, which typically entails the act of simply handing over, as in a package or a correspondence. The word "contribute," meanwhile, implies giving of ourselves and seeing that our gift is appreciated.

In order to make it even more obvious why this concept – this crucial mindset-driven behavior – is the third element necessary in enabling joy in work, consider when proper contribution doesn't occur. Think about those times when teams developed great ideas, great plans, great prototypes, and great products, only to see the value they created get lost in bureaucratic red tape, die in the morass of political maneuvering, or just sit on the shelf as hostages to poorly balanced limits on priorities, capital, time or courage.

Stop and really consider that for a second. It's a sobering thought. But it's one that should motivate you.

As a leader, you're the barrier buster. You're the one the others look to when it comes to providing the crucial link necessary to push the created value toward its contribution phase and therefore cycle right back to connectivity. And that is what will enable joy in work, for you, and for those you lead.

Experts at Enabling Joy

The concept of enabling joy in work is found in the theories of Dr. W. Edwards Deming, Noriaki Kano, and Frederick Herzberg. That's why the next segment is devoted to taking a closer look at these business philosophers as we continue to build the basis of our new and improved on-the-job mindsets.

The Deming Basis

Who is Deming

As stated earlier, my whole journey to understand and live out the enable-joy-in-work calling was triggered by two different sources. One was the Genesis account. The other was the work of Dr. W. Edwards Deming where I first saw the phrase about "joy in work."

The elegant insight in that short phrase can be best understood when we look at the work of Deming, a man born in simple surroundings in 1900, who came to be considered the father of the modern quality movement.

After decades honing his insights on the topics of management and leadership, it was in his final years, still providing help to the world's biggest organizations in his 80s and 90s, that he summarizes his most profound conclusions.

Deming's Philosophy in a Nutshell

This is admittedly going to be a very brief overview considering how long Deming worked and how much he contributed. To truly appreciate his genius and, I daresay, inspiration, please read *The New Economics* or *Out of the Crisis*.

No, they're not easy reads, but they are worth the effort.

Deming was famous for his four-day seminars. It was from these seminars that we hear Deming's statements about driving out fear. He complemented that message with the concept of joy in work. In some of his words:

Joy in Work – Words from Deming

Why are we here? We are here to come alive, to have fun, to have joy in work.

Management's overall aim should be to create a system in which everybody may take joy in his work.

The aim of management, management's job, is to enable everybody to enjoy his work.

Management's job is to create an environment where everybody may take joy in his work.

Now, keep in mind that Deming came onto the American scene in the mid-1980s, when he began admonishing many American managers over their consuming desire for quick and easy recipes. They didn't have or want to have the discipline necessary to become actual chefs, an unfortunate mentality he set about re-educating.

He resisted because it sounded like they just wanted a recipe. However, later he did put together his famous 14 Points, as bulleted in their entirety below.

As you read through them, notice the words in *bold italic*. These are emphases I added since they're key vocabulary incorporated into this book. Also, as you go along, ask yourself: Was Deming just giving advice on improving quality or are these more profound than that?

1. Create constancy of purpose toward improvement of product and service, with the aim to become competitive and to stay in business, and to provide jobs.
2. Adopt the new philosophy. We are in a new economic age. Western management must awaken to the challenge, must learn their responsibilities, and take on *leadership for change*.
3. Cease dependence on inspection to achieve quality. Eliminate the need for inspection on a mass basis by building quality into the product in the first place.
4. End the practice of awarding business on the basis of price tag. Instead, minimize total cost. Move toward a single supplier for any one item, on a *long-term relationship of loyalty and trust*.

5. Constantly and forever improve the system of production and service to improve quality and productivity, and thus constantly decrease costs.

6. Institute training on the job.

7. Institute leadership. (See point 12). The aim of supervision should be to help people and machines and gadgets to do a better job. Supervision of management is in need of overhaul, as well as supervision of production workers.

8. *Drive out fear*, so that everyone may work effectively for the company

9. *Break down barriers* between departments. People in research, design, sales, and production must work as a team, to foresee problems of production and in use that may be encountered with the product or service.

10. Eliminate slogans, exhortations, and targets for the work force asking for zero defects and new levels of productivity. *Such exhortations only create adversarial relationships*, as the bulk of the causes of low quality and low productivity belong to the system and thus lie beyond the power of the work force. Eliminate work standards (quotas) on the factory floor. Substitute leadership. Eliminate management by objective. Elim-

inate management by numbers, numerical goals. Substitute leadership.

11. ***Remove barriers that rob the hourly worker of his right to pride of workmanship.*** The responsibility of supervisors must be changed from sheer numbers to quality.

12. ***Remove barriers that rob people in management and in engineering of their right to pride of workmanship.*** This means, inter alia, abolishment of the annual or merit rating and of management by objective.

13. Institute a vigorous program of ***education and self-improvement.***

14. ***Put everybody in the company to work to accomplish the transformation.*** The transformation is everybody's job.

Summed up, we can view enabling joy in work as being when leaders remove the barriers to workers' abilities to connect, create, and contribute – or what Deming would refer to as removing the barriers that rob people of their pride in what they do.

Quick Takeaways from Deming

1. If you need or want to lead, then your calling is enabling joy in work.
2. This calling is about removing barriers to intrinsic motivation: the main reasons why we do what we do. Notice how it's not about encouraging us to do our best; it's about stopping those actions that demotivate us from doing our best.
3. Joy in work is not the same as making people happy; it's much deeper than that.

The Herzberg Basis

Who is Herzberg

Frederick Herzberg is the author of one of the most request-ed *Harvard Business Review* articles of all time: "One More Time: How Do You Motivate Employees?" A noted psycholo-gist, he's considered to be one of the most influential names in business management. Born to immigrant parents in 1923, Her-zberg spent most of his life doing research on organizations and consulting for them while employed at the University of Utah.

Herzberg's Philosophy in a Nutshell

If you want the best way to understand his philosophy, you're best off reading that *Harvard Business Review* article referenced above. But for those who can't find the time to do so, here's my translation...

In essence, we all have intrinsic motivation. Studies show that the hardest lessons the average human ever learns in life are how to walk and talk, neither of which provide any extrinsic rewards at the time. We do it because we're intrinsically motivated to make such advancements. So clearly, there's something to this kind of drive.

It's highly important to keep that in mind. Look back at Deming's 14 Points. Notice that points 7, 8, 10, 11 and 12 speak about removing or ceasing certain practices. That's because they're all barriers to intrinsic motivation.

Herzberg states that what we normally think of as motivators are not. They're "dissatisfiers." We're talking pay, benefits, offices, bonuses, and fancy titles here. Yes, believe it or not, those are dissatisfiers.

Human beings are rarely satisfied with what we have. We usually want more, whether because we think we deserve it or because we think it will make us happier. Recognizing this, Herzberg's claim is that we need to bring those outlying factors to a point where they're only minimally dissatisfying.

That's important, so let's restate it: The goal is to just get pay levels, job benefits, office sizes, bonuses, and titles to a point of minimal dissatisfaction. These factors – which are called "hygiene factors" by Herzberg – never become satisfiers and they never become motivators. They don't have that capability. They're always going to fall into the dissatisfier category because sooner or later we will want more. Now here's where it's a little tricky; when you cease to have any dissatisfiers, it isn't as if you achieve satisfaction; you only achieve a lack of dissatisfaction. And the same applies to motivation.

Herzberg's model is comprised of two coinciding routes or realities. On the one hand, there is the path toward minimizing dissatisfaction. On the other is the path toward allowing intrinsic motivation to do its magic. He claims we can take action to minimize dissatisfaction. Just like we can take action that will block intrinsic motivation.

Herzberg basically states that no person or group really ever motivates someone else into behaving better. We either remove dissatisfiers, which may seem like extrinsic motivation; or we remove the barriers to intrinsic motivation. And it's this concept of removing barriers that *Enabling Joy* is built on.

Admittedly, this can be confusing. Since pictures are supposed to be worth a thousand words, I created the following to serve as a visual story and better explain Herzberg's theory.

We have two curves and they are concurrent. In other words, you can be minimizing dissatisfaction and increasing motivation at the same time. The trick is to realize these are not the same.

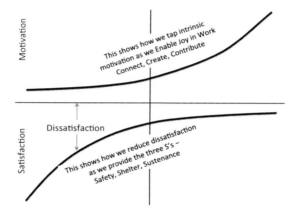

The lower curve is all about minimizing dissatisfaction via what Herzberg calls the hygiene factors. These are factors such as providing more pay, more benefits, and more job security. These hygiene factors, which I refer to as the three S's - Safety, Shelter and Sustenance, only minimize dissatisfaction. These do nothing for motivation.

Why the shape of that lower curve? It sends the message that more you pour into those three S's, the less you get. It's called diminishing returns. In other words, doubling pay does not double how much dissatisfaction is reduced. It also shows that after those S's reach a certain level, providing more actually doesn't do much at all in terms of reducing dissatisfaction. So to restate a previous point, the best we can do is achieve a point where we are only minimally dissatisfied.

The upper curve is all about motivation. Later we will call this enabling joy, but hold on for that. It shows that when we tap intrinsic motivation, or, more accurately stated, when we remove the barriers to intrinsic motivation, we motivate. We enable joy.

The shape of that curve is actually the opposite of our lower curve. The shape shows that even small steps to tap intrinsic motivation provide ever-bigger joy. It's called increasing returns, because each incremental increase yields an even bigger return. The shape also shows that enabling joy is a journey of limitless potential. To put a twist on the words of a popular song, while you can't get no satisfaction, you can always enable more joy.

Quick Takeaways from Herzberg

1. Leading is about looking at what you're doing. If you're minimizing dissatisfaction (sometimes referred to as extrinsic motivation), expect quick, short-term wins that decrease over the long term. If you motivate by enabling joy, expect unlimited possibilities.

2. Look for where there are barriers to intrinsic motivation. Work on removing them to unleash the natural motivation within.

3. You can do both! Minimize dissatisfaction AND enable joy in work. Just always remember that, in so doing, you're achieving two very different – but complementary – outcomes.

The Kano Basis

Who is Kano

Noriaki Kano developed a model that breaks down the various dimensions of customers' wants and needs. Born in 1940, he's a professor emeritus at the Tokyo University of Science and author of *Guide to TQM in Service Industries*.

Kano's Philosophy in a Nutshell

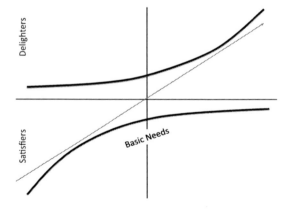

Kano's model provides a sociological perspective to complement Herzberg's psychological one. In other words, Kano looked at the difference between what it takes to satisfy customers versus delighting customers, not employees. Derived in part from Herzberg, Kano put his theory on a graph to explain the dual needs of satisfaction and delight. It was Kano's graphical approach that I then adapted to Herzberg's model.

Kano's upper curve, called the delighter (also referred to as attractive quality) represents the increasing gains from efforts designed to excite your stakeholders. The lower curve, meanwhile, is what Kano positive spun as the satisfier or "must-be quality." It represents the reality that, at best, you can only reduce dissatisfaction to a minimal amount by giving the customer what they expect and meeting stated specifications.

The gray diagonal line
In a typical Kano Model, the diagonal is referred to as one-dimensional quality or the performance attribute. It accounts for situations when more is better. In the context of enabling joy in work, that dimension is accounted for in the upper line.

Quick Takeaway from Kano

1. Delighting a customer is very similar to enabling joy in work. In that case, helping customers connect with a product or service, see how that product or service helps them create value and to make that value useful to what they see as important in life would help unlock how to delight the customer.

Quick Takeaways from the Dual Curves
(looking at both Herzberg and Kano)

1. The curves give us a predictive view of our actions, showing us the probable paths of doing more satisfying versus doing more motivating or delighting.
2. Realize how all the problem solving and pothole patching in the world can only minimize dissatisfaction.
3. Realize that the upper curve, which we call enabling joy, is a path of limitless potential.

Toolkit for Enabling Joy

L et's get to work putting this all together. This section is how I weaved together all the thoughts from the creation and nativity accounts in the Bible, along with the insights of Deming, Herzberg and Kano. These are where I take all that philosophical, maybe even theological, stuff and put it into practical use.

The goal is to convert all this great sounding theory into a tool, a tool that can show us how well we are enabling joy and how we could change our daily priorities to put more energy into enabling joy while not losing sight of our responsibilities as managers.

Remember Assumption #1: Leading is about the people; managing is about the work. Managing the people and leading the work actually looks like it works in the short term, but the long term consequences are disastrous.

Start With the Dual Curves

That top curve is all about your job of leading, enabling joy. That bottom curve is all about managing the work.

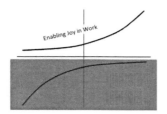 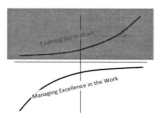

This gives us a meaning along the vertical axis, so now let's look at meaning for the horizontal axis.

As with most graphs, we will use the horizontal axis as a way to think about actions with respect to time. Notice that the vertical axis is in the middle of the graph, not along the left. We are going to put that to use.

We are going to differentiate our actions with respect to time based on actions that address the past and actions that address the future.

This would give us the left side for actions that we take reactively. That's not as in an emotional reaction but rather actions that respond to issues that have already happened.

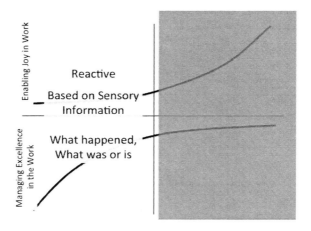

With the left being for reactive actions, that gives us the right for proactive actions. Those are the things we do to affect the future, that we do proactively.

I like to think of that left side being like pothole patching and the right side being building new highways.

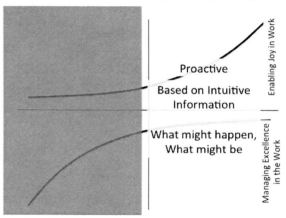

Now let's take a deeper look at those top and bottom halves.

The bottom half is driven by what I'll call logical decision processes. With respect to working with people, these
are the actions that address the three S's – safety, sustenance and shelter to minimize dissatisfaction. With respect
to working with processes and products, these are the
actions that address the making the that product or process
defect free, to drive out the dis-satisfiers.

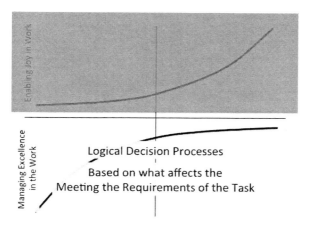

The top half is driven by what I'll call the relational decision processes. These are the actions we take to improve

the way we connect, create and contribute. From a people perspective, it's what we do to open up ways to be better at the three C's. From a product or process perspective, these are the actions that improve how our processes or products emulate best practices, delight the customer or set a new standard.

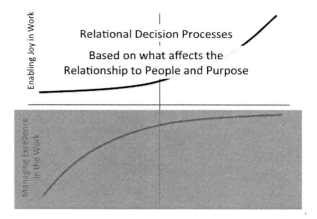

A Map for the Enabling Joy Journey

Here's our overall map. Let's take a look at this map quadrant by quadrant.

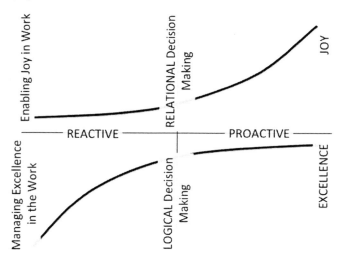

Reactive Excellence

Let's start by looking at that lower left.
Managing Excellence, Reactively.

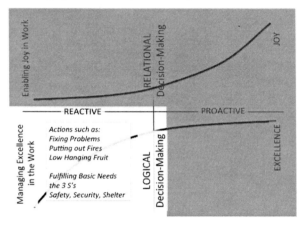

This is area of the map depicts actions such as classic problem-fixing, firefighting, and pothole patching. Something is wrong, and we need to fix it. Obviously, there's great value in performing these tasks, which create solutions to problems. That is why the curve in the area shows a sharp decrease in dissatisfaction, as we find solutions to those things that are causing dissatisfaction.

The shape of the curve in this part of the map also explains the old process-improvement adage about getting the low hanging fruit, where we got lots of benefit at the start but, after we pick those low hanging fruit, the effort seems to go up while the benefits seem to taper off.

Up Is Good
The area under the horizontal should most correctly be stated as dissatisfaction, and moving up is less dissatisfaction. Many people call moving up an increase in satisfaction. That makes a similar point, and if that is easier for you, then use that terminology. The reason I state it as less dissatisfaction is because it reminds us that having zero dissatisfaction is actually not the same as having satisfaction, it's just no dissatisfaction.

Thinking of it in light of its Herzberg basis, it's when we move from working without pay or benefits to working with pay and benefits. That's a big jump in reducing dissatisfaction. To illustrate what the curve is showing, take this pay example another step. Moving from good pay to better pay seems like it would reduce dissatisfaction yet again. And it does, but not nearly to the same degree. In other words, we have a diminishing return for our cost.

When we lead events or institute plans that are largely about correcting what went wrong or what is wrong, the results will behave as shown by the curve. More importantly, these actions are very necessary for managing, but they are not joy enablers. We will only reduce dissatisfaction.

Proactive Excellence

Move on to the lower right.

Managing Excellence, Proactively

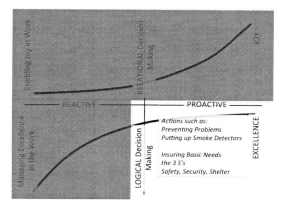

This is where our actions are intended to prevent future problems. Since we don't have the problem now, these only offer us an extra dose of less dissatisfaction.

It's sort of like buying car insurance. It makes driving a slight bit more enjoyable by removing that nagging worry reasonable people have about how they'll afford the costs incurred due to an accident. Yet car insurance doesn't reduce the actual likelihood of the accident. The reality is that while you may be fully insured, you haven't eliminated worrying that someone is going to put a wrinkle in your new car.

Let's take a look at the shape of the curve here. Notice that it is fairly flat. What this means is that lots of effort will yield a benefit, but in almost an unnoticeable way.

This is where we frequently get misled. These predictively corrective actions do not decrease dissatisfaction commensurate with the effort to do them. Having lots of insurance or lots of risks with mitigation efforts is comforting in a way, but doesn't reduce dissatisfaction (also seen as frustration, worry, discontent) compared to the energy we put in.

Now, don't be misled. I heartily endorse buying insurance. It's a very necessary activity along the same lines as scheduling in early roadwork to prevent potholes, and installing smoke detectors to prevent loss due to fire. This is the realm of excellence management that, when done well, separates success from failure. Yet even when it's as successful as possible, it's still not the source of joy.

Keep in mind, this curve shows dissatisfaction and is not a return on investment curve. In other words, we are talking about dissatisfaction, not fiscal management.

Reactive Enabling Joy

Now, the upper left quadrant.

Enabling Joy, Reactively

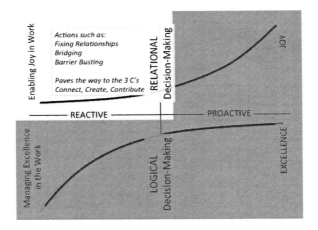

This is area of our map that reflects how we enable joy when we reactively respond in ways to help our people connect, create, and contribute. At its best, this area of the map describes our actions to help our people believe that he and she are not alone and not out on a windy corner. This is where we make sure our people don't see themselves as anonymous or irrelevant. This is where we build bridges by mending broken relationships. In this mode, we break down barriers to creativity and contributing, usually in the forms of organizational fear of change and bureaucratic red tape. In a marketing context, it's those actions we do to keep up with our competitors and the marketplace. In a planning context, it's about staying connected by revising our purpose to be more relevant or adjust to changes in prevailing needs.

It's reactive in that these actions enable joy by responding to the current condition, as opposed to creating a desired future condition.

For as wonderful as this facet of enabling joy is, notice the shape of the curve. We get benefits, but at first they are almost unnoticeable as depicted by the flatness of the curve. We should not be looking for instant leaps in enabling joy. But here's the cool news. The more we do, the more we get as that curve shows increasing joy. This is what makes the reactive enabling joy actions so appealing.

They build on themselves. Actions in this quadrant may seem inconsequential at first, but they act like your money in the bank- the interest builds on itself. Fixing a relationship may seem like just a quick "I'm sorry" but it leads to the ability to connect, and then create, and then contribute.

This area of the map describes those leadership actions that create better connectedness, especially by way of renewing team member relationships, getting a system view of how people relate to customers, stakeholders, executives, and, as depicted by the fable, challenges from a board of directors.

Proactive Enabling Joy

Finally, the upper right
Enabling Joy, Proactively

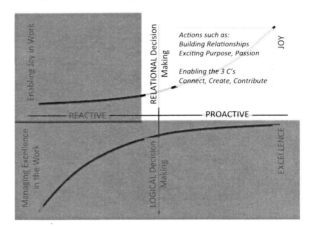

Look at the shape of the curve here. That upward sweep describes an unleashing of potential, an increasing release of each person's innate motivation to connect, create, and contribute. The actions described here are when we as leaders find new ways to connect our team to each other, to customers, and to our vision. It's a connectedness that transforms the work at hand into a passion rather than a chore to finish. These are the leadership actions that transform changing a diaper from a stinky job into a precious moment of connection and comfort with your child.

This area of the map includes actions that help the team more effectively create and contribute value, like improving work processes by unleashing productivity and creativity, delegating decision-making, and removing roadblocks.

Let take delegating decision-making as an example to illustrate the enabling joy power described by that rapidly increasing curve. By delegating decision-making up front, a foundation of trust is needed. If as a leader you feel uncomfortable with doing this proactively, i.e. before you are forced to by other factors, then you see that you need to build better connection. When you proactively delegate that decision-making, you make a vast difference in connecting people to purpose. Why? Because now they need and want to own the decisions and hence the increased connection. Delegating the decisions makes them think of what impacts will occur to others, unlike the passive reactive thinking that accompanies a passed down decision. This builds camaraderie of decision owners. This, in turn, drives ownership of the processes that the team will use to create the value, be it a product, process, solution, idea, or a changed diaper.

With this ownership, there is now the potential to truly con-tribute that value to a customer. (The hyphen placement in con-tribute is hopefully reminding you what the word really means). Hopefully, you can see how all of these build on each other. The build on each other in a growing way that would be described in math terms as logarithmic. A simpler way to picture this is how a tree grows; each shoot creates branches that create more shoots, more branches.

The message here is straightforward.

As a leader, this proactive enabling of joy should be your operating zone. The more time and energy you put into these types of actions, the more you will be enabling joy.

Putting our Map to Use

Time Priority Assessment

Are you properly balancing the leadership role of enabling joy in work with the management role of providing consistent excellence?

The following set of steps will give you a way to quantify that balance or imbalance, working on the assumption that the best indicator of priority is where you put your precious time. You can do this individually or you can do this as a leadership team, as happens in the fable. The benefit of the team approach is that it will reveal what the cultural norms are, not just individual decisions.

Your goal is to roughly quantify what fills your week and see if you are balancing your roles of leader and manager. This is an assessment to see where your practiced priorities really are.

We'll walk through it a step at a time. But keep in mind that this is my suggested approach. You should be ready to adapt it to your organization and team scenario.

Step 1: Start with a clean version of the curves. Just draw a version on the whiteboard or a poster chart.

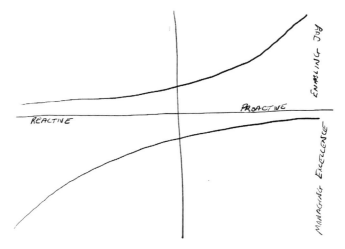

Step 2: Look back at your work calendar(s) over the last couple of weeks or month, making sure you're reviewing at least 80 hours' worth of data. The more, the better.

Now ask yourself what's on that calendar? The answer is almost assuredly lots of what I'll call events: meetings, appointments, happenings, reading, writing, talking, doing... Develop a tally of all the events and the approximate time spent on each. This is not a billable hours sort of accuracy, just a way to get an idea of the time you spend on each.

Step 3: Clump the list of events into related categories. The list below offers a suggestion on generic descriptions for those categories. Feel free to develop your own but be sure to think across the nature of all four quadrants on the map.

1. Fixing problems (schedule, material, money...)
2. Preventing typical problems
3. Analyzing non-typical problems
4. Generating ideas
5. Sharing knowledge or networking
6. Identifying risks, including "black swan" events
7. Mitigating risks
8. Improving or analyzing processes
9. Experimenting or prototyping
10. Aligning (prioritizing) the to-do

11. Aligning our team (search for common ground)
12. Improving or mending relationships among people
13. Mentoring or coaching
14. Goal-setting and/or visioning

Step 4: For each category, add up the hours that you spent in that area.

For example, on Friday, I spent two hours in a meeting resolving a problem my company had with a broken part. Since we've seen this kind of issue often, there wasn't really any analysis so this would fit into category No. 1: fixing a problem.

Also on Friday, I found that I spent an hour on the phone with a team member who was complaining about what another member hadn't done. I was mending fences, so I see that as fitting in No. 12.

On Monday, I spent an hour helping one of my team members see where the team was going and why he's still critical to what we're accomplishing. That could be mentoring (No. 13) or goal setting (No.14), but it was really more about alignment, so I put that hour with No. 11.

I also clumped No. 10 and No. 11 together since I usually do both of these at the same time at morning meetings and meetings with upper level management. Here's my completed list.

1. FIXING PROBLEMS — 25
2. PREVENTING TYPICAL PROBLEMS — 15
3. ANALYZING NON-TYPICAL PROBLEMS — 6
4. GENERATING IDEAS — 6
5. SHARING KNOWLEDGE / NETWORKING — 2
6. IDENTIFYING RISKS — 1+5 $^{talk}_{to Bob}$ = 6
7. MITIGATING RISKS — 3
8. IMPROVING / ANALYZING PROCESSES — 8 $^{- include}_{meeting stuff}$
9. EXPERIMENTING / PROTOTYPING — 2
10. ALIGNING OR PRIORITIZING To-Do's — ⎤
11. ALIGNING the TEAM / COMMON GROUND — ⎦ 20 $^{most}_{morning meeting}$
12. MENDING RELATIONSHIPS — 4
13. MENTORING / COACHING — 1
14. GOAL SETTING / VISIONING — 2

As you compile your list, expect to clean up some of your thoughts and pile designations to some degree but remember that this is intended to be a quick assessment. Trust your instincts. No need to turn this into a science project. This advice is even more critical when doing this as a leadership team because you don't want to get paralysis by analysis.

Step 5: After adding up the totals for each type of event, sort that list by how much time spent. Again, this is not an academic exercise; it's a way to see where we spend our time. To that end, I suggest clumping the pile into thirds; the third you spent the most time on, the third you spent the least time on and the third left that's in the middle. The advice of thirds is just a rough idea and reflects common phenomenon. It may break into quarter, quarter, half; that's okay. Three piles is the advice.

For the pile you spent the most time on, make a note card or sticky note for each. Print it in bold, dark ink.

For the pile you spent the least time on, make a note card for each. Print it in light, thin ink or a pale color.

For the pile, make the note for each in a color or boldness that is distinguishable from your other two.

(I like using colors: Black for the third of most time, orange or yellow for the third of least time and a light blue or green for the middle group)

FIXING PROBLEMS
PREVENT TYP PROBLEMS   } MOST
ALIGNING TASKS/PEOPLE   TIME

IMPROVE/ANALYZE PROCESSES
IDENTIFYING RISKS
GENERATING IDEAS
ANALYZING NON-TYP PROBLEMS

Mending Relationships
mitigating Risks
Networking   } LEAST
Experimenting/Prototyping TIME
Visioning
Mentoring/Coaching

Step 6: Put those notes on our map. Discern what each activity is really about. Think in terms of the language used to describe each of the four parts of our map:

Top half: Enabling Joy – reactively and proactively

Bottom half: Managing Excellence – reactively and proactively.

Now transfer each note to its place on the map.

Admittedly, this is easier to see through a graphic. Below, you'll find how I'd arrange my activities. Keep in mind that this is my interpretation and you're going to have to work it out for yourself. Thinking this through on your own or with your team is a key part of the assessment.

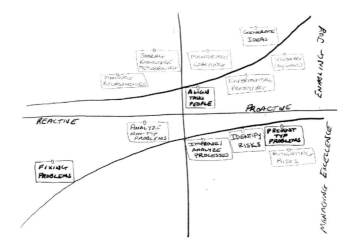

Notice that I stuck the "Align Tasks People" note (that also includes "Prioritizing") in the upper right but near the middle. That reflects that I know that in that category I saw activities that were really all of the four areas at once. That's okay. I am going for speed and rough estimating here. For me, these would include meetings where we establish priorities and revise project schedules. A people thing, they're mostly about building beliefs, connecting team members, and helping to ensure value creation, all of which should automatically make them an act of enabling joy.

Step 7: Stand back and take a look. If doing this as a team, have a conversation about what you see. The big question to answer is whether you see your time as being well balanced between enabling joy and managing for excellence.

The answer is *your* answer, not a textbook answer.

Can you see whether your time and energy are going where they need to go? Remember to pay attention to the shape of the curves. Problem solving always looks good in the short term with its big wins. Enabling joy may look like it's not giving you results in the short term, but...

A Word on Metrics

Some thoughts for an enabling joy dashboard

Are you properly enabling joy? We have this great advice and the question is whether we can see how well, or even if, we are enabling joy. Here are some ideas that can help.

1. **Time Priority Assessment** – As described above, this is the go to metric, because it shows where you spend your time. If enabling joy doesn't show up over the course of 80 hours, that would be cause for concern.

2. **Customer Delight** – If you're not enabling joy at work, there's a very good chance you're not delighting customers either. In service industries, where your production people are in direct contact with your customers, this is most likely a highly correlated metric.

3. **Employee Engagement Surveys** – It's exceptionally helpful to make sure you're asking questions about pursuing dreams as much as whether there are good benefits. Don't confuse joy with satisfaction.

4. **Turnover Rate** – Enabling joy in work should translate, of course, into having joy in work. People who enjoy their work don't typically leave. As such, the turnover rate is the primary indicator on the level of connectivity achieved, both to the people in the organization and the purpose of the organization.

5. **Speed to Market** – This should reflect how well people are able to create and contribute value. It indicates whether the joy component is stopping short after connectedness has been achieved.

6. **Project Performance** – This should reflect how well all three C's are working. Note that the critical component of project management is communication.

7. **Risk/Opportunity Realism Check on Projects** – Did predictions match outcomes? One way or the other, this is an indirect measure of how well team members foresaw their ability to connect, create, and contribute.

8. **Vision Check:** Was the vision achieved on a per-project or per-product basis? If the answer is yes, you next want to assess how the ability to connect, create, and contribute helped realize that vision.

Your Journal

In the end, this is all just a fun book and a nice theory until you choose to accept enabling joy as your calling as a leader. So now it's time to answer some questions aimed at getting you actively living that calling. My guess is that if you picked up this book, you already are on the road to making yourself a better leader. Now take some time to make this improvement journey visible. Let's write it down. Take your time. Find a trusted peer to talk to about what you have written.

What is YOUR calling as a leader?
(I think it's enabling joy… but now it's your turn.*)*

What are you currently doing or not doing to increase your team members' ability to connect with each other and to their collective purpose?

How are you specifically helping your people to increase their ability to create value?

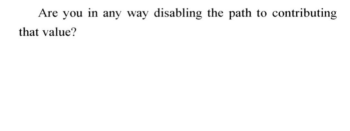

Are you in any way disabling the path to contributing that value?

What will YOU CHANGE to be better at enabling joy?

References

(listed alphabetically by author except for Pope Francis)

1   Pope Francis. The Joy of the Gospel, Image, 2014.

2   Achor, Shawn. The Happiness Advantage, Crown, 2010.

3   Amen, Daniel G. Change Your Brain, Change Your Life, Crown, 1998.

4   Briggs, Isabel. Gifts Differing: Understanding Personality Type. Myers-Davies-Black Publishing. 1995.

5   Deming, W. Edwards. The New Economics, The MIT Press, 1994.

6   Deming, W. Edwards. Out of the Crisis, MIT Press, 1982.

7   Deming, W. Edwards. The New Economics for Industry, Government, Education, 2nd Ed., MIT Press, 1994.

8   Flynn, Vinny. The Seven Secrets of Divine Mercy, Mercy Song and Ignatius Press, 2015.

9   Gaitley, Michael. The 'One Thing' Is Three: How the Most Holy Trinity Explains Everything, Marian Press, 2013.

10   Greenleaf, Robert. The Servant as Leader, pamphlet, The Greenleaf Center for Servant Leadership, (2015).

11   Heath, Chip and Heath, Dan. Switch: How to Change Things When Change is Hard, Crown Business, 2010.

12   Herzberg, Frederick, (1968). "One More Time: How do You Motivate Employees?" (Reprint R0301F), Harvard Business Review.

13   Johnson, Spencer. Who Moved My Cheese?: An Amazing Way to Deal with Change in Your Work and in Your Life, Putnam, 1998.

14   Joiner, Brian and Streibel, Barbara. The Team Handbook, Joiner, 1996.

15   Kahnemann, Daniel. Thinking Fast and Slow, Farrar, Straus and Giroux, 2011.

16   Kelly, Matthew. The Dream Manager. Hyperion, 2007.

17   Kotter, John. Leading Change, Harvard Business School Press, 1996.

18   Lencioni, Patrick. Five Dysfunctions of a Team, Jossey-Bass, 2002.

19   Lencioni, Patrick. Three Signs of a Miserable Job, Wiley.

20   Maxwell, John C. The 21 Irrefutable Laws of Leadership: Follow Them and People Will Follow You, Nelson, 2007.

21   Neave, Henry R. The Deming Dimension, SPC Press, 1990.

22   Pirsig, Robert M. Zen and the Art of Motorcycle Maintenance, 1974.

23   Patterson, Kerry; Grenny, Joseph; McMillan, Ron; Switzler, Al, Crucial Conversations, McGraw-Hill Education, 2011.

24   Pyzdek, Thomas. The Complete Guide to the CQM. Quality Publishing, 1996.

25   Senge, Peter. The Fifth Discipline: The Art & Practice of The Learning Organization 2006.

26   Senge, Peter et. al. Fifth Discipline Fieldbook, Crown Business, 1994.

27   Sinek, Simon. Start with Why: How Great Leaders Inspire Everyone to Take Action, Portfolio Trade, 2011.

28   Walton, Mary.The Deming Management Method, Perigee Books, 1988.

29   Walton, Mary. Deming Management at Work, Perigee Books, 1991

Ode to Joy – **Words** by Henry J. van Dyke

(to the tune of Ode to Joy composed by Beethoven)

Joyful, joyful we adore Thee, God of glory, Lord of love
Hearts unfold like flowers before Thee, opening to the sun above
Melt the clouds of sin and sadness, drive the dark of doubt away
Giver of immortal gladness, fill us with the light of day

All Thy works with joy surround Thee,
earth and heaven reflect Thy rays
Stars and angels sing around Thee, center of unbroken praise
Field and forest, vale and mountain, flowery meadow, flashing seas
Singing bird and flowing fountain, call us to rejoice in Thee

Thou art giving and forgiving, ever blessing ever blessed
Wellspring of the joy of living, ocean depth of happy rest
Thou our Father, Christ our Brother, all who live in love are Thine
Teach us how to love each other, lift us to the joy divine.

ABOUT THE AUTHOR

Paul Armstrong has spent over 30 years in business process improvement and problem solving, and has been active on committees in church organizations, youth sports and scouts. A long time Deming aficionado, Paul has long been curious about the mandate to enable joy. In 2006, he founded eNthusaProve, LLC to coach and consult with teams to enthusiastically achieve amazing results. Paul speaks on topics ranging from leading change to knowledge management, but he is especially passionate about enabling joy. Paul, an alumnus of the U.S. Merchant Marine Academy with an MSIE from Pitt, resides in Lancaster, PA with his bride of over 35 years, and a joyful chocolate lab.